The
My Lai Cover-Up

Deceit and Incompetence

by

Major General Ira A. Hunt Jr.,
USA (Ret)

Prologue

The most publicized single incident of the Vietnam War was the My Lai 4 massacre when on 16 March 1968 a company unit of the Americal Division while conducting its first combat assault in South Vietnam massacred over 400 innocent civilians, raped women, bayoneted livestock and burned down houses in the hamlet of My Lai 4. There were numerous reports of this "insane act of violence."[73] Aviators flying that day, reported troops indiscriminately shooting and seeing over a hundred non-combatant bodies; the Village Chief reported 570 civilians killed; and the Viet Cong later distributed leaflets that portrayed Americans killing "500 people who had empty hands." On the other hand, the assaulting unit reported it had been in a contested battle where 128 VC had been killed and that there had been no indiscriminate shooting. By the next day the command section and the general staff of the division had been apprised that a large number of non-combatants had been killed. The serious disconnect between the two reported assault outcomes had to be investigated by the Americal Division headquarters and the results reported to higher headquarters. However, due to the lies and false reports of the two assault leaders, investigations failed to determine the extent of the killings. Unbelievably, not a single non-combatant casualty was ever reported by the Americal Division and the situation remained unknown for over a year until a former soldier, Ron Ridenhour, sent a letter to the Secretary of Defense alleging what had occurred.

The letter created a public furor and the Department of the Army directed the Peers Inquiry to determine the facts relating to the My Lai assault and to report on its findings. The inquiry cited thirty persons that it believed had committed reporting or investigative offenses, none of whom were punished and only Col. Henderson, the brigade commander, was court-martialed. The report of the Peers Inquiry is considered the authoritative source of information about the My Lai Incident. A major finding of the Inquiry states that actions were taken at every level of command of the Americal Division to suppress information concerning the war crimes committed, which unfortunately has been interpreted to mean a systematic cover-up occurred. This finding reflected badly on the integrity of the Army and it will be shown that it was an incorrect conclusion.

The local Vietnam situation is updated and the heinous war crimes committed by the participants are vividly described. The reporting of the My Lai assault to the Americal Division Headquarters and the subsequent actions taken by it, including the receipt of investigative reports, are discussed in detail. Also, for the first time, an explanation of **how** the bold cover-up was orchestrated by the two lower-level combat commanders who, concerned that their orders had been misinterpreted, desperately attempted to suppress knowledge of the extent of the massacre. Their efforts succeeded because of "incredible mismanagement" by the division's senior leaders who were responsible for investigating the incident. This book answers many of the perplexing questions concerning the My Lai incident which have arisen over time.

Also discussed is why, interestingly, no one in the Americal Division was ever convicted for failing to report a single civilian casualty to higher headquarters as required. Disconcerting to some is that although many members of Charlie Company committed war crimes, only one, Lt. William Calley, was convicted of crimes against humanity.

TABLE OF CONTENTS

THE LETTER AND THE INVESTIGATION

In late March 1969, Mr. Ron Ridenhour, who had served as a soldier in Vietnam in 1968 sent a letter (see Appendix A) to the Secretary of Defense and the Congress of the United States about atrocities that he heard had been committed on an operation by Charlie Company, First Battalion, 20th Infantry a unit in Task Force Barker, a battalion of the 11th Light Infantry Brigade in the American Division.

Ridenhour's letter stated he had heard from a wide variety of soldiers that "something rather dark and bloody" had occurred in March 1968 at a village called "Pinkville" in Quang Ngai Province of the Republic of Vietnam. "Pinkville" was a notorious area that seemed to be infested with booby traps and enemy soldiers. In the latter part of March Task Force Barker moved out with the mission to destroy the trouble spot and all its inhabitants. He was told that 2nd Lt. Kally (Calley) of Charlie Company 1/20 had rounded up several groups of old men, women and children and machined-gunned them. He was further informed that not only had Charlie Company received orders to slaughter the approximately 400 inhabitants of the village but that these orders had come from higher up in the chain of command. Ridenhour was convinced that something very bad had indeed occurred and he felt that a widespread public investigation should be made.

Ridenhour's letter caused a furor in Congress and at the Defense Department. The scope of the alleged atrocities in Ridenhour's letter was difficult to believe. If they were true it is almost inconceivable that they could have remained unknown for such a long period of time. General William C. Westmoreland, the then current Chief of Staff of the Army, had been the commander of forces in Vietnam at the time of the referred to incident and he was greatly disturbed by the content of the letter. He had been briefed in April 1968 shortly after the operation of Task Force Barker, and had been given no indication that Vietnamese civilians were involved in any way, much less that atrocities had been committed.[1]

Ridenhour's letter, which was based on hearsay, initiated an intensive Department of the Army investigation into the facts of the matter. Initially the Army requested Headquarters US Army Vietnam to provide any and all information it could find concerning the operations of Task Force Barker at the time referred to. The headquarters responded that there indeed had been a successful operation against the hamlet of My Lai 4 on 16 March 1968 during which 128 combatants had been killed but there was no evidence of atrocities having been committed. This was the first indication of a potential cover-up. To delve more deeply into the affair General Westmoreland directed in late April 1969 that the Army Inspector General conduct a preliminary investigation to ascertain the facts.

The preliminary investigation commenced about thirty days after Ridenhour's letter was dated and was conducted by Col. William V. Wilson. The investigation consisted of substantiating or not the allegations of the intentional killing of non-combatants and the destruction of property which were contained within the letter. Col. Wilson located the persons referred to in Ridenhour's letter and interviewed them. Travelling throughout the country he interviewed thirty-six witnesses over a two months period to determine what had happened, trying to separate authorized combat actions from criminal acts. Col. Wilson's report in July 1969 indicated that there was sufficient evidence that criminal acts had been committed.

Therefore, the Department of the Army initiated two separate and concurrent investigations; one to determine those who may have committed criminal acts at My Lai, and the other to determine why the atrocities at My Lai had not been reported by the Americal Division. Considering criminal acts, the responsibility for additional investigations was transferred to the Criminal Investigation Division of the Army Office of the Provost Marshal General. The CID immediately encountered two major problems. First, by July 1969 many of the enlisted men who had committed war crimes in March 1968 had completed their tours of duty, been discharged from the service and were now civilians. The Department of the Army could have transferred their cases to the Department of Justice for prosecution, but chose not to do so. Second, most of the Charlie Company individuals who had committed war crimes were claiming they were just following the orders of their superiors. It will be shown subsequently that there was some validity to their reclamas. In determining the war crimes, illegal orders were the most vexing and serious problem. As the result of its investigations charges against thirteen personnel suspected of committing war crimes were referred to LTG Albert O. Connor, Commander of the Third Army at Atlanta, Georgia for disposition. After a thorough review, four of them were court-martialed and only one, Lt. William Calley Jr., was convicted. Calley, a major participant in the war crimes committed at My Lai 4, was charged on September 5, 1969, with six specifications of premeditated murder for the deaths of 104 Vietnamese civilians near the village of My Lai 4. At his trial the military prosecution contended that Calley, in defiance of the rules of engagement, ordered his men to deliberately murder unarmed Vietnamese civilians. In his defense, Calley claimed he was following the orders of his immediate superior, Capt. Ernest Medina. The court-martial jury convicted Calley on March 29, 1971, of the premeditated murder of 22 Vietnamese civilians and he was sentenced to life imprisonment and hard labor at Fort Leavenworth. At the time many in the American public disagreed with the verdict and believed the sentence was too harsh. Ultimately, the sentence was fully commuted after Calley had served three and a half years of house arrest in his quarters at Fort Benning.[106]

Considering the failures to report, General Westmoreland, noting that none of the identified criminal acts and war crimes had previously surfaced, was very concerned that there could have been a possible cover-up of information by persons involved with the incident. Therefore, he appointed a well-respected senior military officer, Lieutenant General William R. Peers, to head an exhaustive investigation into any previous reports and investigations of the My Lai 4 incident[2]. The directive for the Peers Inquiry states that the scope "does not include, nor will it interfere with, ongoing criminal investigations in progress". Further that it "will include a determination of the adequacy of the investigation(s) or inquiries on this subject, their subsequent review and reports within the chain of command, and possible suppression or withholding of information by persons involved in the incident". Obviously there had been a cover-up of the assault and the task of the Inquiry was to determine how and why the cover-up was successful.

The interrogation of witnesses by the Peers Inquiry began on 2 December 1969. Although there was no statute of limitations for those crimes allegedly committed at My Lai 4 there was a two year statute of limitations for those military offenses associated with reporting, negligence, improper performance of duty, failure to properly investigate and so forth. The clock had been running and any charges that were to be brought for military offenses had to be filed prior to 15 March 1970. This was a very short time to complete such a complex endeavor. Notwithstanding, the Peers Inquiry expeditiously obtained a tremendous amount of information concerning what happened at My Lai 4. Through extensive interrogations they talked to over 400 people and they obtained a large number of documents to supplement the testimonies obtained. They also travelled to South Vietnam to visit major US headquarters to peruse their files and to visit My Lai 4 on the ground.[105] In all no stone was left unturned.

Once the incident at My Lai 4 became known publicly it was only a matter of time before recently discharged perpetrators would begin to talk openly, probably to relieve troubled consciences, and an Army photographer would attempt to cash in on his vivid photographs of murdered women and children. Just as the inquiry was commencing, Life Magazine on 5 December 1969, published an article on the Vietnam Massacre at My Lai 4 which included graphic color pictures taken on the operation which the magazine had purchased from Mr. Haberle, as well as interviews with soldiers who were there. The article created a public furor. People were appalled viewing the stark color photographs of the atrocities and many were concerned that such incidents could have been kept unreported. At the time there was also interest by Congress and hearings were being planned. It was obvious that the pressure was on to determine the facts so that the Army could report its' unvarnished findings to the American public.

The Peers Inquiry completed its report on 14 March 1970, thereby meeting the statutory deadline. Caught up in the emotions of the times it cast a wide net, producing a list of thirty persons who, it felt, had known of the killings of non-combatants and other serious offenses committed during the My Lai 4 operation, but had not made official reports, had suppressed relevant information, had failed to order investigations, or had not followed up on the investigations that were made.[2] The Army Office of the Judge Advocate General was appointed to review the sufficiency of evidence obtained by the Peers Inquiry and to prepare court-martial charges against the individuals cited. As a result, court-martial charges against twelve military officers alleged to have committed military offenses were forwarded to LTG Jonathan O. Seaman, Commanding General of the First US Army, Fort Meade, Maryland, who had general court-martial jurisdiction. General Seaman after his own evaluation and upon the advice of his staff judge advocate further dismissed five cases for lack of sufficient evidence. Therefore, charges against seven officers were served and they were subjected to Article 32 investigations to again determine if the charges preferred could be substantiated and if so should they be sent to a general court-martial for trial.

An Article 32 hearing is a proceeding under the United States Uniform Code of Military Justice, similar to that of a preliminary hearing in civilian law. "No charge or specification may be referred to a general court-martial for trial until a thorough and impartial investigation of all the matters set forth therein has been made" to determine whether there is enough evidence to merit a general court-martial.[3] Offenders in the US military may face non-judicial punishment, a summary court-martial, special court-martial, general court-martial, or administrative separation. The commander directing an investigation under Article 32 details a commissioned officer as investigating officer who will conduct the investigation and make a report of conclusions and recommendations. The investigating officer will, generally, review all non-testimonial evidence and then proceed to examination of witnesses. The defense is given wide latitude in cross-examining witnesses.

Included in the seven Article 32 investigations were the two key chain of command officers, MG Samuel W. Koster, Commanding General of the American Division who directed investigations to be made, and Col. Oren K. Henderson, Commanding Officer of the 11th Infantry Brigade, who conducted the investigations. These two officers were charged primarily for investigative failures. The other five officers (Maj. Calhoun, Maj. Gavin, Maj. Guinn, Maj. Watke, and 1st Lt. Johnson) were charged with reporting failures concerned with the operation and with advisory responsibilities. Subsequently, all of the officers undergoing investigations for reporting failures had their charges dismissed for lack of sufficient evidence.

On 5 August 1970, the author who had recently completed a thirteen month tour of duty in Vietnam as Chief of Staff of the 9th Infantry Division with two periods as a brigade commander was directed to investigate the charges against Col. Oran K. Henderson who as brigade commander was in a pivotal position in the chain of command and was charged with one specification of dereliction of duty in that he willfully failed to conduct a thorough and proper investigation of allegations or reports of excessive killing of non-combatants, and a confrontation between a helicopter pilot and ground forces; and one specification of failing to obey a lawful general regulation, MACV Directive 20-4, dated 27 April 1967, in that he did not report to his Commanding Officer incidents and acts thought or alleged to be war crimes, the intentional infliction of death or injury upon non-combatant Vietnamese civilians, both in violation of Article 92, Uniform Code of Military Justice; as well as being charged with two specifications of giving false official statements with intent to deceive before the Peers Inquiry. Henderson's Article 32 investigation not constrained by time and utilizing all of the evidence obtained by previous Army investigations thoroughly delved into the reporting situation and it provides a comprehensive insight into the totality of the reporting and investigative actions taken in South Vietnam, which is one of the subjects of this book.

A finding of the Peers Inquiry with respect to suppressing information stated:

> "At every command level within the Americal Division, actions were taken, both willingly and unwillingly, which effectively suppressed information concerning the war crimes committed at Son My Village."

For the past forty years many have interpreted that finding to mean that a systematic cover-up of the incident occurred at every level of command in the Americal Division. For example, Thomas Ricks, the author of the best selling "The Generals", relying on that interpretation states "it was a modern low point of Army generalship, and of the Army itself." [113] Those are harsh words impuning the integrity of the Americal Division senior officers and as Ricks has stated "the Army itself." The reputation of the Army requires the clarification of the finding -- which this book accomplishes.

This book analyzes how LTC Barker master-minded the bold cover-up which began almost immediately during Charlie Company's assault. It relates how he and Capt. Medina, the assault commanders, were able to successfully direct the attention of the brigade and division commanders to what they falsely claimed to be a contested assault where a large number of VC were eliminated and twenty non-combatants were unfortunately killed, instead of having the senior commanders focus on the hundreds of civilian casualties reported by the division aviators and the Vietnamese. Their cover-up succeeded because of the incompetence of those receiving the reports and investigating the My Lai 4 incident. Even though the two junior assault commanders were aggressively suppressing information of the massacre, it will be shown that there was not a division-wide suppression of information relating to the assault.

Everything about the aforementioned Charlie Company combat assault is astounding – the massacre itself, the reporting of the incident and the follow-up investigations. Over 400 innocent old men, women and children were brutally killed and the My Lai 4 hamlet totally destroyed. How could a company of average young men have absolutely lost their cool? The perpetrators immediately instigated a cover-up of the atrocity. Although the deaths of many non-combatants were reported almost immediately to the heads of all the major US and Vietnamese units in the area, news of the rampage was bottled up within the local geographical area for over a year. The Viet Cong fully exploited the incident by widely distributing propaganda leaflets meant to embitter the rural population. The American and Vietnamese who received the relatively factual communist leaflets considered them unbelievable because "American troops … would not do something like that". But they did – violating all regulations about the treatment of civilians and property.

This book answers several of the perplexing questions that have arisen since the My Lai 4 incident was publicized, such as:

> What caused the breech of good order and
> discipline by the soldiers of Charlie Company
> which led to the massacre of Vietnamese civilians?

> How did the Vietnamese officials react to the
> reports they received of the massacre?

> Why weren't non-combatant casualties reported
> by the Americal Division to higher headquarters?

> How could information about the My Lai 4
> atrocities have been effectively covered-up for
> over a year?

> Why wasn't the division headquarters able to
> determine the full extent of the killings?

> Why weren't Americal Division officers punished
> for failing to properly investigate and to report the
> incident?

A BROAD UPDATE

Since the war in South Vietnam occurred some fifty years ago it is considered essential to provide a broad update concerning the general circumstances affecting US forces in the country at March 1968 to include: the importance of pacification; the units involved and their leaders; geographic locations; and the overall security situation.

Pacification

The avowed goal of the North Vietnamese Communist insurgency in South Vietnam was to control the maximum amount of land and numbers of people; first, for the political cachet this control brought to their claims of sovereignty, and second, for the support it brought to their military operations. South Vietnam was an agrarian society in which most of the population lived in rural areas, dependent upon agricultural production to eke out a meager living. Many of the peasants were tenant farmers, illiterate, medically ill cared for, sometimes plagued by corrupt officials and often taken advantage of by greedy landlords. The rural peasants were the least privileged of Vietnamese society, and the most susceptible to Communist indoctrination preaching class warfare. The countryside was the primary target of the Communist insurgency, and conversely, the pacification of the rural area became the major goal of the GVN, which desired to bring security and economic and political stability to the country.[4] Pacification was the End-Game!

The Communists were well organized, with a multi-tiered structure to take and maintain control of the rural villages and hamlets. At the apex of their structure were the well-trained and experienced Viet Cong and North Vietnamese main force units. They were supported in combat operations by local force units, which generally operated near their homes where they knew the terrain and people. The main and local force units provided the cover for the guerilla forces, which were also localized and whose responsibility it was to support the combat units by transporting supplies, constructing defenses and providing intelligence as well as conducting harassment and sabotage actions. The guerillas were a primary source of manpower for communist combat units. Finally, a vital cog in the communist hierarchy was the Infrastructure, which at the grass-roots level collected taxes, provided intelligence, and assisted in recruiting. All elements were supported by a well-honed propaganda organization whose activities took advantage of the people's discontent.

In the early 1960's the Communists were gaining control of most of the countryside. Rural area pacification was of vital importance to the GVN, but it focused its pacification efforts in the mid-1960's primarily on population centers and provincial and district capitols—the "oil blob strategy" whereby the GVN intended to expand its control outward from these nuclei, ultimately reclaiming all of the countryside. This was prudent; for at the time the GVN had neither the means nor the organization to effect control of the thousands of villages and hamlets. Since the GVN units had generally withdrawn into population enclaves, the communists pretty much had the run of the countryside. Their control of the abundant resources and manpower of the rural areas gave the communists the ability to attack the GVN urban strongholds, and the military situation was rapidly deteriorating. It was at this point, in 1965, that the United States sent in troops to try to stabilize the situation.

By mid 1967 security in South Vietnam had not yet stabilized. Rural areas were the decisive battlefields where the major ideological struggle with the communists was ongoing. It was crucial in this ideological, economic and military struggle to win the allegiance of rural peasants.

To facilitate pacification the Government of South Vietnam established a Ministry of Revolutionary Development which coordinated the activities of the various governmental activities involved in the all-important pacification program, thereby ensuring cohesively organized efforts.[5] The Americans established the office of Civil Operations and Revolutionary Development Support (CORDS) in May 1967 in order to unify US pacification activities. South Vietnam's forty-four administrative provinces were subdivided into a variable number of districts and CORDS provided an American advisor to the Vietnamese chief of every province and district to assist in pacification matters. In addition to the CORDS system, the US assigned military advisers to all major Vietnamese units down to the battalion level to advise and assist RVNAF units in all areas of operations and pacification.

Pacification was a complex process requiring the coordination and cooperation of Allied military forces and GVN civilian ministries. It entailed three distinct stages: establish security (military), this was generally accomplished by either U.S. or ARVN units driving off the VC main and local force units; stabilize the situation (political), this occurred when territorial and National Police units were able to purge the hamlets of VC

15

guerillas and infrastructure and GVN cadres were able to operate and establish political institutions; enhance development (community development), this included provisions of health and educational facilities, initiation of social welfare programs, establishment of land tenure, et cetera.[6] In establishing security it was essential to protect the rural population.

The first two steps in the pacification process could just as well apply to communist efforts to gain control by driving off Allied military units and stabilizing the situation with local forces and guerillas, allowing the VC infrastructure to establish a political apparatus. Control was not an irreversible process—the contest could go either way. That's what the tug of war to control the thousands of villages and hamlets which constituted the foundation of Vietnamese society was all about.

How do you measure or define control? MACV went to great pains to answer that question. It designed the Hamlet Evaluation System (HES) to assess monthly the effects of insurgency upon the people of Vietnam[7]. Essentially, it permitted a set of questions to be asked about the people and their environment and evaluations to be derived from the responses. The system provided information in all three areas—military, political and community development—through a set of 165 multiple-choice questions. HES data originated at the level of 12,000 hamlets and villages with information gathered monthly from various sources. The HES was designed to meet several objectives, the most important of which were to monitor the progress of the pacification effort throughout South Vietnam and to provide a geopolitical profile of South Vietnam. Broadly speaking, hamlets and villages were considered either under GVN control, communist control, or to be contested.

In Quang Ngai Province in early 1968 many more hamlets were under Viet Cong control than were under GVN control and a large number of hamlets were contested. Song My Village, which included My Lai 4, had been under Communist control since 1964. Consequently for pacification to proceed the security of the area had to be greatly improved. The Vietnamese contributions to Quang Ngai area security was provided by the three regiments of the 2nd ARVN Infantry Division commanded by Colonel Nuyen Van Toan, fifteen regional force companies and seventy-three popular force platoons. Regional Force (RF) companies normally operated within the confines of a province and were more mobile and better equipped than the Popular Force (PF) platoons which operated locally in their districts. The Quang Ngai Rural Development Program was under the control of the province chief, LTC Ton That Khien, who had forty-one revolutionary development teams, half of them were working in hamlets, providing health and educational facilities and initiating social welfare programs.

The three brigades of the American Division were undoubtedly the most potent military forces in the province and they worked closely with the RVNAF to provide the contested hamlets and those under GVN control the essential security umbrella required for the political and developmental activities to be effective in the pacification in the Quang Ngai countryside.

To succeed in pacification efforts it was important that all military forces treat the rural non-combatant population circumspectly. With this in mind, Headquarters MACV early on in the US involvement prescribed policies in 1966 designed to minimize non-combatant casualties, stating that the use of unnecessary force leading to non-combatant casualties will embitter the population and drive them into the arms of the VC, who will then fully exploit such incidents to foster resistance to the GVN and the United States. This was the case at My Lai 4. This policy was followed on 27 April 1967 by MACV Directive 20-4 calling attention to the requirement for following the Geneva Conventions for the Protection of War Victims. MACV Directive 20-4 paragraph 5(a) stated "It is the responsibility of all military personnel having knowledge or receiving a report of an incident or an act thought to be a war crime to make such incident known to his commanding officer as soon as possible."[8] In incidents such as My Lai 4 such reports would follow the chain of command which ultimately meant that Headquarters, American Division would have the responsibility of forwarding the report to is next higher echelon and to Headquarters MACV. The MACV directives clearly spelled policies and procedures to prevent the sort of incidents which apparently happened at My Lai 4.

To ensure a bottoms-up approach for the humanitarian treatment and respect for the Vietnamese people four wallet sized cards were issued by September 1967 to every soldier. They were: "The Enemy in Your Hands", "Code of Conduct", "Geneva Convention", and "Nine Rules". These cards emphasized the responsibilities of military personnel and their relations with the Vietnamese people, particularly with respect to the use of unnecessary force[9].

Thus by March 1968 clear and concise rules of conduct for US military personnel and the vital importance of the pacification program had been fully established. The 11th Light Infantry Brigade had been given several weeks of training in Hawaii as well as comprehensive training in South Vietnam concerning rules of engagement and the importance of proper conduct towards the Vietnamese people. It was important for leaders, particularly those in the lower echelons, to ensure that the rules of conduct were adhered to. The success of the Pacification Program depended on it.

Notwithstanding, all of the regulations and information concerning the safe guarding of the Vietnamese people, the Task Force Barker assault not only failed to engage and drive off enemy troops, thereby permitting the welfare at the hamlet to be upgraded, but it ruthlessly killed the inhabitants. This potentially set back the Pacification Program in Quang Ngai Provence and provided grist for communist propaganda. The attack was an abomination, violating all MACV directives and rules of conduct.

When in July 1969 news of the 16 March 1968 assault was made public in the United States it created a public furor. Newspapers and TV covered the subject for weeks. Congress formed special committees to investigate My Lai and the Army was deeply concerned about possible effects the massacre might have on the successful on-going Pacification Program.

On the other hand, the Vietnamese were concerned that Americans were over-playing the incident. Obviously the GVN was fully committed to maintaining the safety of its people and to the protection of property. However, in those areas under long time VC control local authorities often considered all the population to be Viet Cong. Such was the case in Quang Ngai Provence. Even though the provincial authorities were informed of the assault, they gave the reports little credence and never investigated the incident which was soon forgotten. Generally speaking the Vietnamese were down-playing the incident in order to maintain good relations with the Americans.

The Assault Chain of Command
The My Lai 4 combat assault was conducted by Charlie Company, First Battalion 20th Infantry, a unit in the Task Force Barker Battalion of the 11th Light Infantry Brigade in the Americal Division on an operation in Quang Ngai Province in Military Region I of South Vietnam on 16 March 1968. The background of the units involved and their leaders is discussed subsequently, as well as the concept of the chain of command:

The Americal Division was organized in September 1967. At that time only one of the three separate brigades to be attached was in Vietnam and for a prolonged period it was a task force organization. In March 1968 the division consisted of three light infantry brigades (196th, 198th, 11th) each of which had its own support units. These initially independent brigades were organized so that they could be detached for deployment to higher priority areas, if necessary. It wasn't until April 1969 that the brigades were made fully part of the division. In March 1968 the divisional administrative and logistical functions were still being fleshed out and the division was in the process of publishing regulations and procedures to insure the uniformity of personnel and logistics operations. Major General Samuel Koster was the Commanding General and BG George Young was the Assistant Division Commander for Maneuver. The divisional headquarters was located at Chu Lai and its primary area of operations was Quang Ngai Province.

Koster, born in 1919, was a 1942 graduate of West Point. He served as a battalion commander in WWII and directed the US Eighth Army's guerrilla warfare operations during the Korean War. He was a well-respected officer who after his service in Vietnam was promoted and given the prestigious assignment of Superintendent of the US Military Academy.

The 11th Infantry Brigade was reactivated in 1966 and assigned to the 6th Infantry Division in Hawaii. It consisted of three infantry battalions: the 3rd Battalion 1st Infantry, the 4th Battalion 3rd Infantry and the 1st Battalion 20th Infantry. During 1967 the brigade underwent a series of active training programs to include air mobility, jungle warfare and advanced individual training. In July 1967 the brigade was alerted for assignment to the newly formed American Division in South Vietnam. The brigade faced a serious personnel assignment problem in that over 1300 soldiers were non-deployable to Vietnam because of the twelve month rotational policy then in effect. A constant replacement of personnel continued right up to the deployment date. This played havoc with the brigade training program and the training schedule initiated for deployment had to be shortened from eight to four weeks. Unfortunately, the brigade was still short more than 700 soldiers when it finally deployed to Vietnam.

Because of its truncated training program in Hawaii, MACV stipulated that the brigade would receive a month of additional training in country before undergoing actual combat operations. Upon arrival in Vietnam it received in-country orientation and combat assault and Viet Cong village training under the auspices of the 3rd Brigade 4th Infantry Division. However, as late as February the brigade continued to receive hundreds of replacements in order to bring its units up to strength. Notwithstanding the personal turbulence, BG Andy Lipscomb, the initial 11th Brigade Commander, stated "Of course every commander thinks his troops are pretty well trained, but I think these were exceptionally well trained..."[10]

Colonel Oran K. Henderson, the Executive Officer of the 11th Brigade since March 1967 assumed command of brigade from BG Lipscomb on 15 March 1968. According to Colonel Henderson "I had a normal light infantry brigade, less about 60 people – officers and men – who were forming headquarters for Task Force Barker. I did not have an executive officer. We skimmed off our staff down to the bone to organize and operate Task Force Barker. "[11]

Henderson, born in 1920, enlisted in WWII and fought in Europe as an infantryman where he received a battlefield commission. After the war he reverted to civilian life but subsequently requested and was granted a commission in the Army where he had an exemplary military career. He commanded units at every level from platoon to brigade, fought as an infantryman in three wars, was wounded four times, was decorated with the Silver Star five times for gallantry in action and was chosen three times by senior general officers to be their aide-de-camp.

The Task Force Barker was activated in early 1968 when General Koster directed the 11th Brigade to take over a new area of operations, the Batangan Peninsula, which he considered required a minimum force strength of six infantry companies. The genesis of the battalion was explained by BG Lipscomb, "The only way we could do it before we got our fourth battalion was to form a provisional battalion. I took the best man I had available, which was my S-3, Colonel Barker, Frank Barker, who was later killed, and gave him the provisional battalion. Task Force Barker, I called it. In selecting the companies of this battalion, I knew that I couldn't leave it up to my battalion commanders because, naturally, they would want to give me the weakest companies. Since I had the 1st Infantry, the 3rd Infantry, and the 20th Infantry Battalions, the logical way to do it would be to take Alpha Company of the 1st, Bravo Company of the 3rd, and Charlie Company of the 20th. Colonel Beers would have never voluntarily agreed to let Medina go. It just came out that way because I selected them that way. Those three companies became Task Force Barker and were sent up to the Batangan Peninsula and started on what we code named Operation Muscatine. This was toward the end of January when this started. Then I had, in effect, four bob-tailed infantry battalions working there."[10] The administration of the detached companies, however, continued to be handled by the parent battalions. BG Lipscomb's assessment of LTC Barker was that "Barker was a tough little paratrooper. Not that that makes him tough, but he came up through the ranks and he was hard-nosed himself." In organizing the Task Force an austere staff was drawn from the staff of 11th Brigade. This weakened and reduced the effectiveness of the brigade's staff.

Barker, born in 1928, enlisted in the Army at New Haven, Conn. He performed well as an enlisted man and attended officer candidate school. He was drawn towards airborne activities and became a ranger. He was assigned to the 11th Infantry Brigade in Hawaii where he was the brigade operations officer. Barker was a strong and energetic leader.

Charlie Company, 1st Battalion, 20th Infantry was organized as a standard infantry rifle company with an authorized strength of six officers and 158 men. However the company was generally under-strength and had an overhead of about twenty soldiers who were required to handle administrative and logistical duties at its base area. With attached personnel, the tactical operational strength was only 125 men, requiring some of the platoons to operate with only two squads which was detrimental to unit cohesion.

Captain Ernest Medina had commanded the company almost from its activation in Hawaii. He was considered by all to be an outstanding leader and he was well liked and admired by his troops. He was much older than the average company commander having been a former enlisted man. In Hawaii, Charlie Company had received jungle, amphibious and air mobility training and exercises. The company was proud to have been selected to deploy to Vietnam with the initial group of the brigade on 1 December 1967. This early deployment of the company reduced the period of accelerated training for deployment, which when combined with the disruptive influx of newly assigned personnel degraded the effectiveness of its unit training. A review of the background, attitudes, trainability and educational level of the enlisted men of Charlie Company by the Department of the Army Director of Personnel concluded that there was no significant deviation from the average enlisted personnel of the Army.[12]

Medina, born in 1936, as a sixteen year-old lied about his age in order to join the National Guard where he performed well. After high school graduation he worked in a variety of jobs and in 1956 enlisted in the Army and was stationed in Germany. He was an outstanding NCO and attended the Infantry Officer Candidate School where he graduated in 1964 with honors and was his class battalion commander. Medina was highly competitive and a very strong leader.

LTC Edwin D. Beers, CO of 1st Battalion of the 20th Infantry Regiment from July 1966 to July 1968 stated that comparing the company commanders within the 11th Brigade, Captain Medina would be on top. In fact, LTC Beers rated Captain Medina as the most outstanding captain he has ever seen. He called him a complete soldier who lives for the Army and loves the Army.[13] All of the personnel, including his enlisted men, have rated Captain Medina as an outstanding unit commander. For example, Mr. John H. Small said, "As far as Capt. Medina is concerned, I can only say that, as a commanding officer, I believe he was the greatest. I knew him a long time. He was the best CO anyone could have over there."[14] It is interesting that LTC Beers rates Captain Michles, B/4-3 Infantry, Captain Shelton, B/1-20 Infantry, Captain Medina, C/1-20 Infantry as the top three company commanders in the brigade and both Captains Michles and Medina were the unit commanders of the maneuver elements during the Task Force Barker operation of 16 March 1968.

1st Platoon, Charlie Company:
Charlie Company had three platoons, all of which participated in the combat assault of My Lai 4. Most of the killing of My Lai civilians was done by the 1st Platoon under the command of Lt. William Laws Calley. In fact, Calley himself was the major perpetrator of the slaughter. The 1st Platoon had a strength of 26 soldiers and operated with only two squads.

Calley, born in 1943, after graduating from high school attended Palm Beach Junior College in 1963. He dropped out after receiving unsatisfactory grades and worked in a variety of jobs before enlisting in the Army. After his Advanced Individual Training he applied for officer candidate school from which he graduated at Fort Benning on 7 September 1967 and was commissioned. He was assigned to C Company, 1st Battalion, 20th Infantry Regiment which was undergoing training in Hawaii in preparation for deployment to Vietnam that December. Calley was a weak officer, and a poor leader, much disliked by his 1st Platoon soldiers.

Barker and Medina were such strong leaders that their subordinates, whether out of respect or fear, did not question their illegal orders calling for the burning of houses, killing of livestock and destruction of crops and property of My Lai 4.

It is important to note that in March 1968 the Americal Division was still a task force type organization. The maneuver elements were still getting organized. New regulations and procedures were still being published. Not only was the division not fully organized, but when the 11th Brigade reorganized to provide an additional battalion size unit they reduced the capability of the brigade headquarters so that when Colonel Henderson replaced BG Lipscomb there was in fact no brigade executive officer for the period 15 March to about 10 April. Additionally Task Force Barker operated with an austere staff and a pick up organization with one company from each of the brigade's three battalions. These companies still looked to their parent battalion for administrative support and to Task Force Barker for operational control. Only when one considers the operating companies within Task Force Barker could a complete organizational entity be found and they were under-strength. Additionally both the assistant division commander for maneuver and the 11th brigade commander were assigned on 15 March, one day prior to the My Lai 4 operation. On the plus side, the company commanders of Task Force Barker were all considered outstanding officers.

The chain of command for the combat assault on 16 March 1968 is depicted on the following chart. Incident reports should proceed up the chain of command and orders were generally directed downward from the top.

Chain of Command,
My Lai (4)

Americal Division

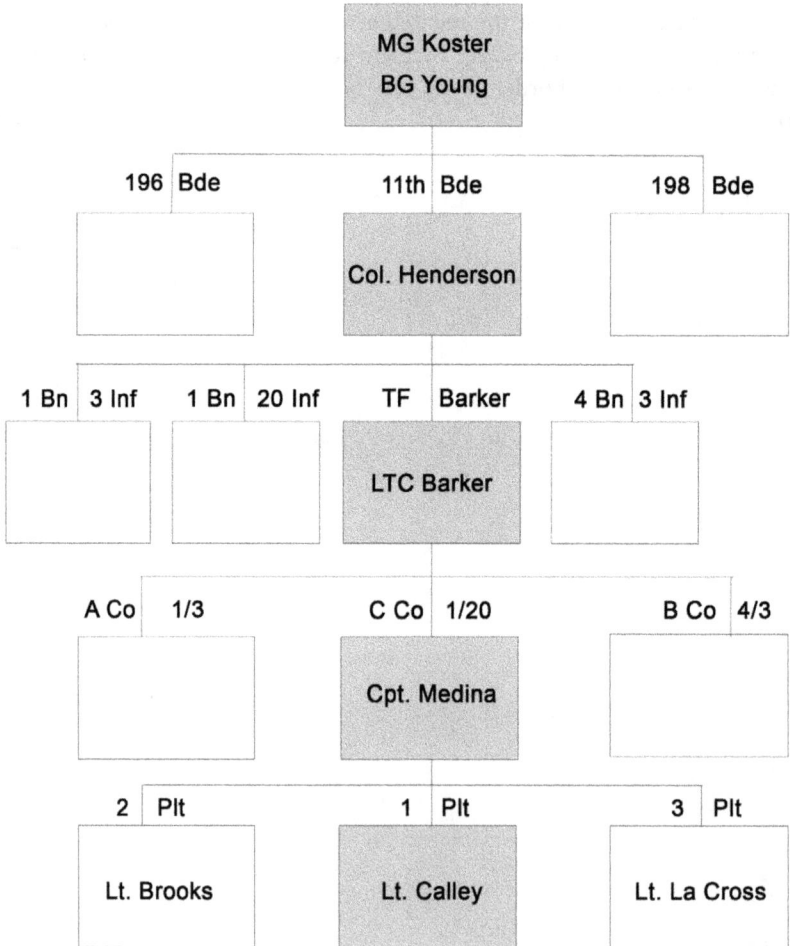

> **MG Koster**
> **BG Young**

196 Bde	11th Bde	198 Bde
	Col. Henderson	

1 Bn	3 Inf	1 Bn	20 Inf	TF	Barker	4 Bn	3 Inf
				LTC Barker			

A Co	1/3	C Co	1/20	B Co	4/3
		Cpt. Medina			

2	Plt	1	Plt	3	Plt
Lt. Brooks		**Lt. Calley**		**Lt. La Cross**	

Geographical Locations

The Americal Division headquarters with three attached infantry brigades was located in Quang Ngai Province. It had a truncated Area of Operations(AO) separated by the 2nd ARVN Infantry Division which had responsibility for the area surrounding Quang Ngai City. Quang Ngai was the southernmost province in I Corps (Military Region 1) located about equal distance from Hanoi and Saigon. The province was bounded on the east by the South China Sea and on the west by the heavy forested mountains of the Central Highlands. Several large rivers drained from the highlands eastward to the sea transporting alluvial soil which created rich delta areas. The beaches of Quang Ngai were renowned for their beauty.

The 11th Brigade's area of operations included the Batangan Peninsula just to the north of the 2nd ARVN Division and the two districts south of the 2nd ARVN Division. Its headquarters was located in the town of Duc Pho. This was a very large area of operations extending 60 kilometers along the coast of the China Sea and about 15 kilometers in width. Because its area of operations was split, it created a more difficult command and control situation, with two of its battalions to the north in the Muscatine AO and two battalions in its southern sector.

Task Force Barker's AO included the eastern portion of the Batangan Peninsula, bounded on the north by the Americal Divisions 198th Infantry Brigade, on the south by the 2nd ARVN Division and on the west by Highway 1, the eastern boundary of the 11th Brigades' 4th Battalion 3rd Infantry Regiment.. Its headquarters co-located with two of its rifle companies was located at LZ Dottie about 12 kilometers north of Quang Ngai City. The third rifle company and a supporting artillery battery were located at LZ Uptight some 14 kilometers northeast of Quang Ngai City (see map 1).

The AO extension required by Task Force Barker for the March 16 operation was obtained from the 2nd ARVN Division and was south of the Dien Dien River which delineated the boundary between Task Force Barker and the 2nd ARVN Division and was in the most eastern part of Son Tinh District which included the village of Son My. Son My Village was known to be a communist stronghold since 1964 and it included four hamlets and several small sub-hamlets one of which was My Lai 4, all of them were highly fortified with bunkers and extensive mines and booby traps (see map 2). According to the Quang Ngai Province chief the VC forces in the area consisted of the 48th Main Force Battalions, the V/20th District Force Company, two sapper companies and approximately three platoons of guerrillas. These units lived with the villagers often working as farmers thus blending with the population only to concentrate and fight as guerrillas whenever they were assured they had tactical advantages.

Son My Village, sandwiched between two rivers had fertile alluvial soil excellent for farming, particularly rice production. It's rural inhabitants were either rice farmers or fishermen, when not engaged in VC activities. My Lai 4, or Thaun Yen, as it was called locally, was a small sub-hamlet in the Tu Cung hamlet, one of the four hamlets of the village. It extended about 400 meters east to west and 250 meters north to south and included approximately 60-70 houses with a population of some 450 inhabitants. Each family had a small plot of land where it planted vegetables and raised pigs, ducks and chickens for sustenance.

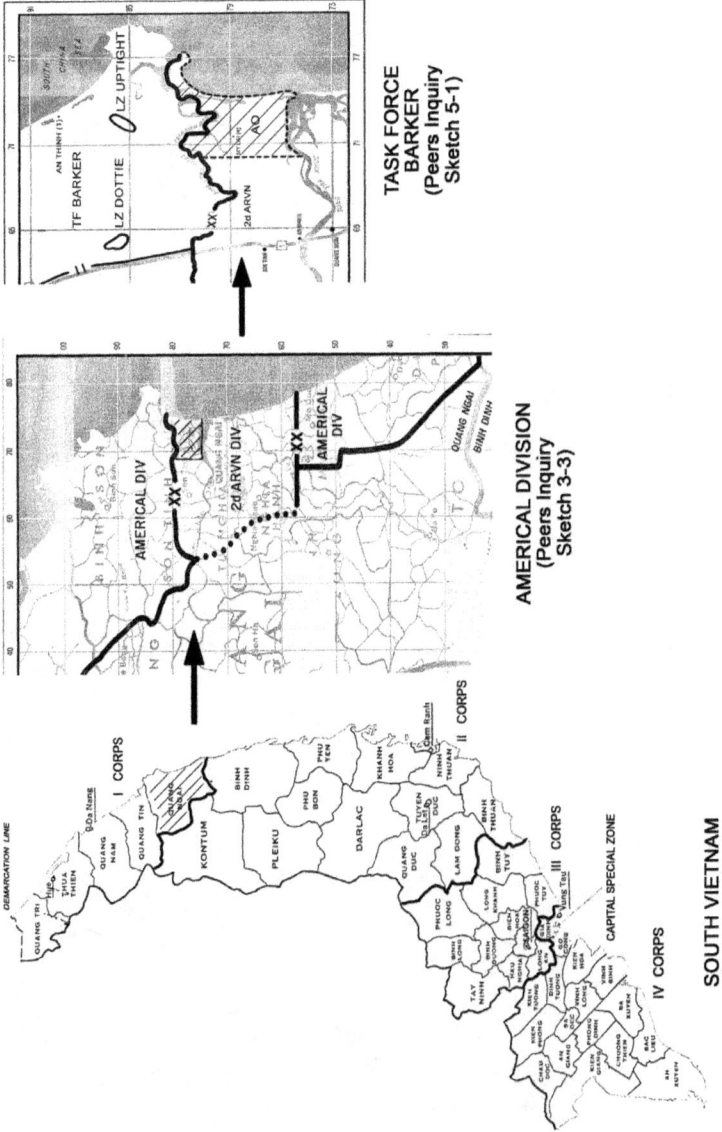

Map 1
TASK FORCE BARKER
AREA of OPERATIONS (AO)

TASK FORCE
BARKER
(Peers Inquiry
Sketch 5-1)

AMERICAL DIVISION
(Peers Inquiry
Sketch 3-3)

SOUTH VIETNAM

MAP 2
Son My Village
(from Peers Inquiry)

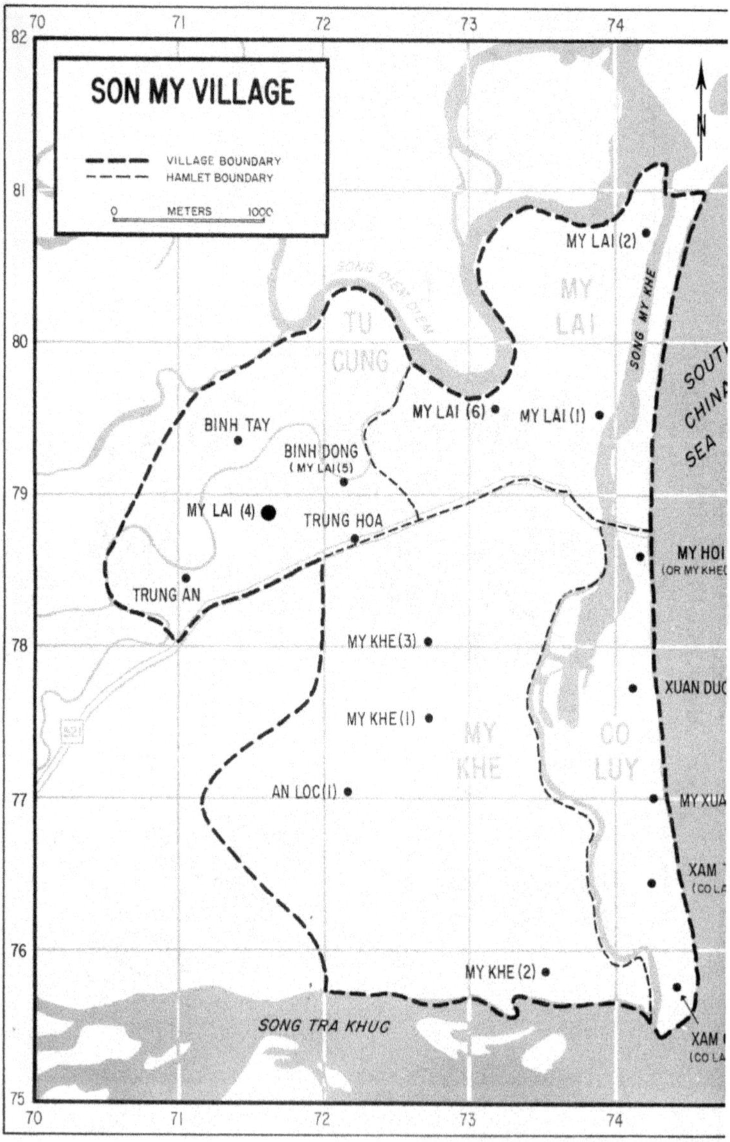

The Overall Security Situation

The North Vietnamese assessment[15] of the 1965-1966 period which they called "Defense Against a Limited War" was "that the Republic of Vietnam Armed Forces (RVNAF) was about to collapse when the allied forces were brought into South Vietnam to save the situation. They no longer considered the RVNAF as a competent opponent and adopted this motto: seek and contain American soldiers, seek and destroy Puppet soldiers. The Communists thought the situation was ripe to defeat the Allies for good by a general offensive. At this time, Communist resolutions and directives were unanimous in their analysis that the RVNAF was so weak that it could not avoid total collapse." Consequently in the 1967-1969 period the North Vietnamese initiated the "General Offensive and General Uprising" phase of the war.

General Westmoreland was acutely aware of the weaknesses of the RVNAF, although it was being upgraded with US weapons and advisory personnel. He realized the urgent need for additional US forces, particularly in the I Corps area, and he had requested additional units to be made available by early 1968. As an interim measure he was relocating brigade sized units to meet the enemy's offensive activities. With respect to those units involved in the My Lai 4 situation this is what he had to say before the Special House of Representatives Subcommittee Son My[9]:

"To complete the picture for you, Mr. Chairman, I believe it would be helpful if I provided some background on those units most directly involved in the Son My incident. Those were the Americal Division and the 11th Light Infantry Brigade ... The 11th Brigade, which had been training in Hawaii, arrived in Vietnam in December 1967 ... I took extraordinary precautions to insure that both the 198th and 11th Brigades were not committed to combat until they were ready. Each of the brigades was placed under the sponsorship of a combat experienced brigade of the Americal until its training was completed. They were then assigned to areas which were relatively quiet in terms of combat activity. I would have preferred additional training time for these units, but a major enemy build-up in the extreme northern area ruled this out. Because of the threat this build-up posed, the 11th Brigade expanded its area of operations".

In 1967, the Communists changed their tactics from company and platoon-sized or smaller operations to battles conducted with multi-battalion attacks. The offensive was to be conducted throughout South Vietnam in several phases by Viet Cong main force units attacking cities and military

units and installations. The Communists believed that with tactical
victories, the people of South Vietnam would rally behind the Communist
cause, thus leading to the overthrow of the government, the so-called
General Uprising.[15]

The first phase of the Communist General Offensive, Tet, was launched on
30 January 1968, when the enemy breached its self-declared Tet holidays
ceasefire to launch countrywide, all-out attacks against provincial and
district capitals and military installations. A significant change in these
attacks by the Communists was the use of daylight assaults on their targets
to include major cities. Using these tactics, they sustained heavy losses.
However, they entrenched themselves in many built-up areas, terrorizing
the populace and inflicting widespread damage to property. Obviously, the
Viet Cong activities were designed to disrupt the economy, thus discrediting
the GVN and convincing the population of VC control.

There were several major ramifications resulting from Tet. The Viet Cong
main force units lost a great number of troops and equipment, requiring
them to withdraw to their base areas to recruit, refit, and resupply. The
attacks on the major cities required the VC Infrastructure to surface in
order to support the offensive, and the VCI as well as local force units were
decimated. The withdrawal of main fore units and the other VC unit losses
left a void in the countryside, enabling the RVNAF to expand their control
outward from the major cities. Additionally, the attacks by the Communists
in 1968, particularly after Tet, alienated the people (just the opposite of the
effect the Communists intended), and the people asked the GVN to
provide them weapons with which to defend themselves. Thus, the
concept of the People Self Defense Force (PSFD) was initiated. These
were local people operating in teams for the most part at the village and
hamlet level. The PSDF expanded rapidly in 1968 and 1969 to over a
million trained personnel who were an important factor in pacification
efforts.[4]

Recognizing the necessity for additional military and paramilitary personnel
to establish governmental presence in support of pacification, the GVN
began to greatly expand and upgrade its Regional and Popular Forces after
Tet. These units were made an integral part of the RVNAF and, as such,
came under the U.S. support program. Not only were their ranks
expanded, but their equipment was appreciably upgraded, with M-16 rifles
and artillery. Also the RF/PF were given the same pay as the ARVN. The
RF, PF, and PSDF were the forces that brought security to the local
population once the Viet Cong main force military units had been
neutralized, which was the responsibility of the ARVN and U.S. forces.

Now the GVN was better organized to expand its pacification efforts and the Program really took off so that by late 1969 over ninety percent of the country was under GVN control.

The Tet Offensive was a major Communist military failure, although it turned out to be a psychological victory in the realm of world opinion. Tet was a definite watershed moment in the war, the US/GVN strategy changed from attriting the enemy to one fully focused on pacification.

THE COMBAT ASSAULT OF MY LAI 4
ON 16 MARCH 1968

What follows is a brief summary of the planning and execution of the operation to include the actions of the various units in Task Force Barker on 16 March. It is not by any means a history of the events, but it is provided to illustrate pertinent actions by units and individuals that have bearing upon the subsequent reporting of the incident and the investigations which ensued.

The Prior Situation In Quang Ngai Provence
During the Tet offensive in the Quang Ngai Province the communists used the 401st Special Mission Regiment and all provincial main force units consisting of five battalions and twelve special mission and local companies to support two NVA regiments of the 3rd NVA Division (Yellow Star) to attack Quang Ngai City. This force was divided into four parts. The Son Tinh District portion of the force consisting of the 48th Local Force Battalion, 107th AAA Battalion, and 506 Alpha Company launched their attack from Son My Village with about 150 villagers and struck at the RF/PF Training Center and the RF Company north of the Tra-khuc Bridge. However, they were defeated by elements of the 2nd ARVN Division and suffered more than 100 casualties, after which they pulled back to Son My Village to reorganize and bury their dead at the village. Charlie Company did not see combat during the Tet Offensive.

Notwithstanding the defeat of the enemy forces at Tet in Quang Ngai Province, the first phase of the General Offensive and the General Uprising had a profound impact on regional pacification efforts. Governmental forces maintained a fear that a second phase of the communist attacks could be forthcoming. Consequently, they did not resume security efforts, but remained in their static defensive locations. This was particularly true for the Son Tinh District which included My Lai 4. Government officials busied themselves in restoring the previous status quo in occupied areas but did not venture back into the long standing VC villages and hamlets like My Lai 4.

Subsequent to Tet, ARVN, RF/PF and Allied forces in Quang Ngai Province conducted a series of operations to relieve enemy pressure. The RF/PF operated in those revolutionary development areas having local village and hamlet authorities and ARVN and US units operated in VC controlled areas with no village or hamlet authorities such as Son My Village which included My Lai 4. BG Lipscomb recalled the 11th Brigade "Had two significant battles in the Muscatine area. Operations against the 48th Local Force Battalion in February which resulted in 74 KIA in the first encounter and 68 KIA in the second engagement in February. I was personally in Pinkville (Son My Village) on about two or perhaps three occasions in February where we'd go in, sweep, have a battle, and then move out. While we were in there I would land. It was a constant thorn in our side because we didn't seem to be able to clean it out and because of the booby traps and mines that were in the vicinity. We'd lost a considerable number of soldiers, I believe. I can't quote figures on this, but they had lower limb wounds in that particular area. It was no question in my mind that Pinkville was one of the toughest nuts we had to crack."[10] The first of these two battles was conducted by Bravo Company on 13 February and the second by both Alpha and Bravo Companies on 23 February. These were the last major offensive actions in the Son My area prior to the 16 March 1968 assault. Charlie Company, unlike Alpha and Bravo Companies, had not yet conducted an operation against the elusive 48th VC Local Force Battalion, although it's time would soon come.

Since it arrived in-country Charlie Company initially assisted in the construction of a base camp at LZ Carentan near Duc Pho in lower Quang Ngai Province. It also received an orientation on the war from the 4th Infantry Division, including instructions on basic patrol techniques, how to call for fire support, and the proper handling of prisoners. A legal team taught it how to distinguish the Viet Cong from non-combatants. This training was very useful since Charlie Company's Vietnam training in Hawaii had been cut short and there had been an influx of recently assigned replacements. Their duties during December included building bridges, digging bunkers and practicing patrol operations. The members of Charlie Company remember this time as most enjoyable with plenty of free time to enjoy the beaches for which Quang Ngai was famous.[107]

On 1 January 1968 the unit came under the operational control of the newly formed Task Force Barker to bring security to the Batangan Peninsula. Charlie Company was to report to LTC Barker on operational matters and to LTC Beers, the commander of the 1st Battalion 20th Infantry Regiment, for administrative and logistical support. Bifurcated command lines are never satisfactory in war time, especially for disciplinary matters. On 26

January the company moved to LZ Dottie, a fire support base in northern Quang Ngai Province, and on 1 February TF Barker was given the task of combing the Peninsula in an all out effort to find and engage enemy units believed to have withdrawn into the area after their Tet attacks. Charlie Company spent several weeks patrolling in the hot, humid climate, searching hamlets and villages for the elusive enemy. Never knowing the VC's whereabouts the company was required to dig in each night to protect themselves. The unit felt isolated and morale fell.[107] The men began to hold the local rural and farming populations in low regard. Some of the men viewed the Vietnamese with contempt, even considering them subhuman.[1] The inability to determine potential enemies from the non-combatant civilian population exasperated the troops.

About mid-February Charlie Company began to take casualties when a 1st Platoon member stepped on a mine. Shortly thereafter the 2nd Platoon received heavy enemy rifle and mortar fire and several men were wounded. The unit could not locate the ambushers to return fire and withdrew under cover provided by gunships. The next day the 1st Platoon was ambushed and a soldier was hit in the gut and died in the field – the first person to be killed in action. This upset many of the men, particularly during the subsequent very emotional memorial service held at LZ Dottie.[107] Charlie Company was taking casualties from an enemy they had never really seen and frustration was mounting. The company was "down in the dumps."[111] Then on 25 February Capt. Medina was leading the company through the countryside when they wandered into a minefield, probably emplaced by Korean forces who previously occupied the area. One explosion followed another as the panicked men tried to extricate themselves. Amongst all of the screams Capt. Medina was calm as he tried to restore order and to effect medical evacuations. Three men were killed and twelve were wounded, several quite seriously. The morale of the unit was shattered. Charlie Company knew fear. Thoughts of revenge against villagers whom they felt were responsible were common. Anger from the loss of their companions led to aggression against the locals by the traumatized soldiers.[108] As the casualties mounted so did Charlie Company's aggressiveness towards the villagers. The soldiers "beat up on Vietnamese on numerous occasions before My Lai 4".[109] At first the acts amounted to manhandling such as striking villagers during interrogations, but they soon escalated into more serious breaches of conduct. One soldier vigorously struck an old man repeatedly, then tied a rope around his neck and hanged him.[110] While questioning an elderly man another soldier repeatedly hit him in the mouth, picked him up and threw him into a well, after which Lt. Calley shot the man with his M-16.[109] Brutality occurred often and the company officers and NCO's did little to prevent it, some even participated in the acts. Both physical abuse and sexual misconduct occurred. During search and destroy missions Charlie Company soldiers often molested village women and in instances committed rape. Moral degradation had set in among several soldiers. On 14 March the popular Sergeant George Cox was killed by a booby trap while on a patrol and two other men were seriously wounded. On their return to base camp angry members of Charlie Company lashed out and shot and killed a civilian woman working in a field.[108]

In a period of just thirty days there had been twenty-eight incidents, mines, booby traps and snipers, without Charlie Company ever closing with the enemy. Six soldiers had been killed and at least eighteen wounded, almost twenty-five percent of the force that on 16 March would conduct a combat assault at My Lai 4 in hopes of finally closing with the enemy which they thought was to be the 48th VC Force Battalion.

The Son My Village area, had been controlled by the VC for many years and was organized into fortified combat hamlets. It was the headquarters of the 48th Viet Cong Local Force Battalion, which drew most of its personnel from local inhabitants recruited right in the area. The 48th Local Force Battalion had been active in Tet and on the two occasions in February 1968 when US forces launched combat assaults against the 48th they met very heavy resistance from the VC occupying the strongly fortified bunker positions. Son My was indeed one of the toughest nuts that the 11th Brigade had to crack.

Planning the Assault
Plans for the 16 March operation were generated at the task force level by LTC Barker who was an aggressive soldier who wanted more or less to clean out his particular area of responsibility. The 11th Brigade log indicates that the Area of Operations clearance was requested on 13 March and was approved on 15 March. The entry citing Col. Henderson's assumption of command of the 11th Brigade was Item 41 in the 11th Brigade log and that the go ahead for the My Lai 4 operation immediately followed, Item 42. Intelligence showed that the operation was being held at the time when women made their major shopping trips to the cities for staples. Since it was market day, LTC Barker felt that women and children would not be in the area.

On 15 March, the day Colonel Henderson assumed command of the 11th Brigade, he travelled to LZ Dottie for a briefing on the My Lai 4 operation. Major Robert W. McKnight, Brigade S-3, filled Colonel Henderson in on the operation in the helicopter on the way from Duc Pho to LZ Dottie. Henderson later said that when he arrived at LZ Dottie he was surprised to

35

find that LTC Barker had on hand all of his company commanders except Captain William C. Riggs. "I walked in and sat down and Colonel Barker stood up and said 'Gentlemen, we are here this afternoon to discuss the operation and Colonel Henderson wants to address some comments to you.' I stood up and discussed my concepts of how infantrymen fight and then I discussed what I knew of the concepts.' So, I don't remember any individual from Task Force Barker standing up and giving an intelligence briefing or briefing of the friendly forces or their employments, other than what I had gained in going up with Major McKnight. I did not receive a formal briefing, in that sense."[17]

Captain Dennis R. Vasquez[18], the Artillery Liaison Officer who planned the artillery prep which was to be a screening device very close to the village, remembers Colonel Henderson saying that if they hit resistance he didn't want them to fall back but to act aggressively. Col. Henderson stated that troops should expect to encounter the 48th Battalion and he wanted the VC eliminated from the area once and for all. In his mind there was nothing unusual about what Colonel Henderson said. It appears that Henderson's presentation on aggressiveness and the need to eliminate the VC from the area once and for all had an influence on his subordinates. Colonel Henderson's statements are the type an aggressive new commander would make to his troops about their first operation under his command.

Captain Eugene M. Kotouc, the S-2 of Task Force Barker, provided the intelligence for the operation. He was an old hand, having been at Quang Ngai Province in 1962. His intelligence reports indicated that the 48th VC Battalion was regrouping after Tet and that the headquarters element and one other unit were supposed to be in My Lai 4. The expected size of the 48th Battalion was more than 200 people. Captain Kotouc stated that intelligence, gained through constant observation, was that non-combatants would be going to market and would be out of the village area by the time of the combat assault.[19]

The 48th Battalion most probably was in the western part of the province refitting and rehabilitating after its heavy losses at Tet. Considering the losses at Tet and the additional attrition by the two Task Force Barker contacts in February it is doubtful that a reconstituted 48th Battalion would have been in the vicinity of My Lai 4. The idea that both Capt. Kotouc and LTC Barker presented that all the non-combatants would have evacuated My Lai 4 was patently not plausible. Even if many housewives went to market, the babies, children, and old folks would have remained in the hamlet. Yet these two facts, the location and strength of the 48th Battalion and the idea of all non-combatants would have evacuated the sub-hamlet by

0700 hours were very important factors influencing the 16 March operation. However, both facts were incorrect. Soldiers were led to believe they would encounter an entrenched battalion of 200-250 Viet Cong at My Lai 4 and that all remaining inhabitants of the hamlet would be VC or VC sympathizers.

In Capt. Kotouc's mind the operation was to be a search and destroy mission. His impression of a search and destroy mission was to search the area and destroy everything in the area once the people had been evacuated. He stated the troops were to burn or blow down houses and kill livestock. Food was to be taken out and the part they couldn't get out was to be destroyed. Capt. Vasquez also recalls the search and destroy mission and stated it would include burning houses.

LTC Barker's concept of the Son My three company battalion operation was to conduct a search and destroy effort to entrap and destroy the 48th VC Local Force Battalion and two additional local force companies believed to be located in the sub-hamlet of My Lai 4. Barker had developed a plan of action that included an air mobile combat assault by Charlie Company into a landing zone just west of My Lai 4 at 0730 hours preceded by a three to five minute artillery preparation. The insertions were to be supported by suppressive fires on the western edge of the sub-hamlet by helicopter gunships. Upon landing Charlie Company was to aggressively move from west to east through My Lai 4. The 174th Aviation Company was to provide a total of nine lift helicopters capable of transporting about sixty soldiers, so two lifts were required. Company B was to conduct the second combat assault at 0830 hours into a landing zone south of My Lai 4, also with an artillery prep. Upon insertion Bravo Company was to be prepared to seal off the eastern edge of My Lai 4 to prevent any enemy from escaping the attack of Charlie Company. Thereafter Bravo Company was to move northward to the vicinity of My Lai (1), (Pinkville) where they would link up with Charlie Company in a night defensive position. Alpha Company was to move by foot from its base area on the evening of 15 March and on the 16th to assume a blocking position north of the Song Dien Dien River to prevent any escape of the 48th Battalion to the north. An aero-scout team from Bravo Company 123rd Aviation Battalion comprised of one OH-23 observation helicopter and two Huey 1B armed helicopters was to screen the area south of My Lai 4 and was to provide observation of the attack. LTC Barker had obtained the support of U.S. navy boats to patrol the coastal waters east of Song My. During his briefing Barker definitely ordered the destruction of homes, livestock, and food stocks. There is no evidence that he ordered the killing of non-combatants.

Barker had crafted a sound operational plan, but it was based on faulty intelligence. Although the Song My operation was designed to last four days, the plan of operations covered only the first day. From an operational view point the unit tactical movements were designed to entrap and hopefully eliminate the 48th Battalion using the coordinated efforts of Task Force Barker and supporting elements. It is important to note that the Song My operation was a battalion endeavor. LTC Barker's subsequent after-action report included the activities of all his units, which was a major factor in sublimating the atrocious actions of Charlie Company during the first hours of the assault.

Capt. Carl Edward Creswell, the division artillery chaplain, was at the Task Force Barker tactical operations center at the time the operation was being discussed. Capt. Creswell asked where Pinkville was. "I was then shown a village on the map by LTC Barker, which I know now as being Song My, which includes My Lai 4. LTC Barker said that a company would be inserted in a combat assault the next day, and if the US troops received any return fire the village would be leveled. I replied, I didn't think we made war that way". LTC Barker then stated, "It's a tough war."[20]

After the meeting, LTC Barker took his company commanders and the artillery battery commander for aerial reconnaissance over the My Lai 4 area. At that time Capt. Medina stated Barker told him he wanted the hamlet destroyed. It is not possible to verify LTC Barker's alleged instructions because he was killed in Vietnam on 13 June 1968.

Col. Barker, the aggressive, airborne soldier, gave orders understood by all that this was to be a search and destroy mission and that everything in the area was to be destroyed, and houses burned. Capt. Medina testified that Col. Barker stated that he had the approval of the senior District Advisor to burn the village. This led Barker's subordinates to conclude that the operation had the approval of higher headquarters and that the search and destroy mission was legal.

Capt. Medina called his company together for a briefing on the 15th just after funeral services for Sergeant George J. Cox, a popular member of Charlie Company who had been killed by a booby trap or mine out in the field on an operation. He told them "We were going into Pinkville and all the children and women would be out of the village at approximately 0700 hours. [21] Everything that was in the village would be VC or VC sympathizers. He expected the LZ to be hot because the elements of the 48th VC Battalion was in the area." Pvt. Thomas Kinch[22] remembers Capt. Medina starting the briefing off by saying, "You all know that happened about two weeks ago but we have a chance to go back tomorrow at Pinkville." Pvt. Kinch says that Capt. Medina said they were to kill all livestock and burn all hooches. Nothing was to be left living but ourselves. Nothing was said about women or children except that everyone was VC or VC sympathizers. The company was going in there to destroy the village and everything within the area including humans. He understood that Capt. Medina wanted every man, woman, or child in the village to be killed.

According to Capt. Medina[23], he gathered his company to issue an operations order. He told them that the estimated strength of the 48th VC Battalion located in My Lai 4 was somewhere between 250 and 280, and we would probably be outnumbered fairly close to two to one. So he emphasized aggressiveness in closing with the enemy to ensure that they did not by pass any bunkers or any enemy positions without thoroughly checking them first. He was definitely sure that the company would make heavy contact that morning and would probably take heavy casualties. Using a stick or a shovel he drew the outline of the landing zone on the ground and where the village was located and said that the 1st Platoon would be utilized as the assault platoon. It would take the right-hand side of the village sweeping the enemy out to the open area on the east side of the village. The 2nd Platoon would sweep through the left-hand side of the village. The 3rd Platoon would be utilized as a reserve platoon, and they would provide rear security at the landing zone and could be committed on the right or left of the village. It would go through and search the bunker complexes, the tunnels, the houses, for weapons, equipment and whatnot in the village. (see Map 3)

Discussing his instructions, Capt. Medina mentioned the briefing at LZ Dottie, "The brigade commander, Col. Henderson, was there and he stated that in the past two operations the failure of the operations was that the soldier was not aggressive enough in closing with the enemy." Capt. Medina went on to say he did not receive any instructions concerning what do to with any civilian population. He was told there would be no civilian populace in the village. He thought the destruction of the village and livestock had been cleared by Lt. Col. Barker with the ARVN senior district advisor of the province.

Many of the enlisted men vividly remember Capt. Medina's briefing. James H. Flynn[24] said "we were supposed to get everything that moved; women, children, cows and pigs, anything that was out there." SSG L.G. Bacon[25] squad leader 2nd Platoon recalls "He told us we were going into the My Lai area and that the 48th VC Battalion had established headquarters there and was operating from this village; and that we were to kill all the VC and

NVA, VC sympathizers, and the animals; destroy all the food; and burn the hamlet down to keep them from living in those quarters again." Sgt Max D. Hutson,[26] squad leader 2nd Platoon said "Capt. Medina called the company together and explained the mission to us. He stated that My Lai 4 was a suspected VC stronghold and that he had orders to kill everybody that was in the village. We did not expect to find anyone in the village and when we did, we did as ordered." The same type of recollections are attested to by others.

Specialist Herbert L. Carter[27], the soldier who allegedly shot himself in the foot and was the only wounded from Charlie Company on the 16 March operation, remembers: "The night before the operation Capt. Medina gave the unit a pep talk and a briefing. The briefing was the usual; equipment to take and what order we would go in. The pep talk was unusual. He said, 'Well, boy, this is your chance to get revenge on these people. When we go into My Lai 4, it's open season. When we leave, nothing will be living. Everything is going to go.' He also said 'to level the village.' Several of the enlisted men were all psyched up as a result of Capt. Medina's briefing and considered the operation an opportunity to get revenge for those members who had been killed in the area previously.[17]

The senior personnel who heard Capt. Medina's instructions found no fault with them. However, the enlisted personnel interpreted them to include the killing of all villagers, creating the impression of possible illegal orders. Polygraph tests later proved Medina did not envision the indiscriminant killing of non-combatants.

The background of orders could also be important when one reviews the attempts of Col. Henderson to obtain information during his investigation. For it is entirely possible that once the field commanders saw that their orders had been misinterpreted and a massacre took place that they would be anxious to cover-up rather than to level with their new commander.

Thus the stage was set for the first combat assault of Charlie Company, 1-20th Infantry. Capt. Medina's company up until that time had had no face to face contact with the enemy. Charlie Company was relatively new in country. There were no combat veterans amongst them. So it is important to note that for the men of Charlie Company this was going to be their first combat assault.

Charlie Company Headquarters
Capt. Medina's actions during the operation are discussed subsequently. C/1-20 Infantry was picked up from the LZ Dottie about 0715, 16 March

MAP 3
Charlie Company Scheme of Maneuver
(from Peers Inquiry)

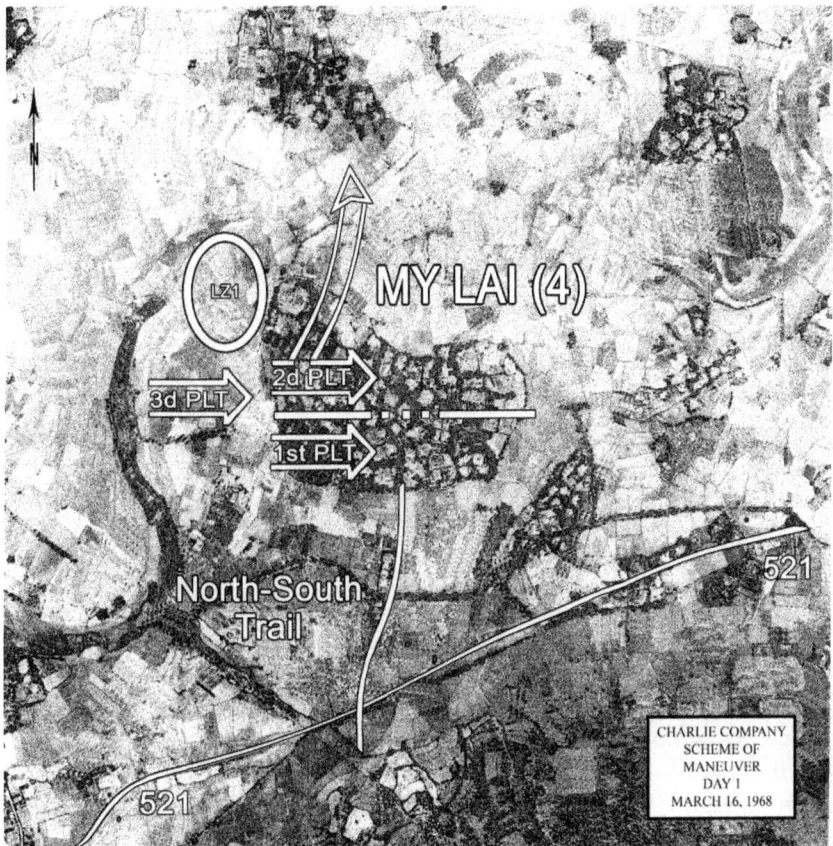

1968 and as the helicopters approached the landing zone (LZ) Capt.Medina
could see the artillery being placed onto the village. The artillery was lifted
as they started the final approach and the gunships initiated their run in for
the suppressing fire. The landing zone was cold. He only had 100 or 105
people. When the last lift was in on the landing zone, the 1st and 2nd
Platoons started proceeding through the village. The 3rd Platoon took up a
security position on the west side of the LZ. Medina moved from the
landing zone to the west side of the village which was the east side of the
landing zone and that's where he established his command post. The 3rd
Platoon was going to follow through and was instructed by him to burn the
village.

Medina noted "There was one helicopter, an OH-23, with one pilot and
two machine gunners, one on each side, that was popping smoke in various
areas throughout the area indicating where there were more VC with
weapons. The pilot said there was a VC with weapon and as I approached I
noticed that it was a woman and there was no weapon. I turned around
and I started to leave and, as I turned around, I saw her arm starting to
move and the first thing that went through my mind was she either has a
weapon or hand grenade and you darn fool you've turned your back on her
and you've had it. I immediately spun and fired two shots. I assume, I do
not know, that I killed her. Then we began moving back toward the village,
approximately 800 meters away."

About noon the company was out in the open area on the far side (east) of
the village, and Medina told them to hold up, set up security and take a
lunch break. He recalls that on the southern side of the village there
appeared to be a group of possibly 20 to 24 men, women and children that
had been killed on the pathway there. There was one small child at the
intersection that had been hit in the stomach with his intestines protruding
out.[23]

Subsequently Capt. Medina falsely told Col. Henderson that he obtained his
non-combatant body count from reports by his platoon leaders and that the
total number of non-combatants killed by the whole company was twenty
to twenty-eight. He reported them to have been killed by either artillery or
gunships and denied there was indiscriminate small arms firing.

Capt. Medina recalls that during his movement through the village Maj.
Calhoun, the Task Force S-3, notified him that he had received a report
from a helicopter pilot who thought some innocent civilians had been shot
and killed. Calhoun told him to make sure that this was not being done.

On reviewing the combat assault Capt. Medina stated that his first report of enemy casualties would have been somewhere between 0800 and 0830 and was 15. The total number reported for Charlie Company was about eighty-five to ninety. He didn't report civilian casualties at that time. After he had married up with Bravo Company in the night defensive position somewhere between 1530 and 1600 hours "Maj. Calhoun asked me for – he wanted to know how many civilians had been killed. I told him that I did not know exactly. He said I want you to move back into the village and get a count. I want to know how many males, how many women, and how many children are dead in that village. And I told him that due to the time and the distance that I did not recommend moving back from my location to the village to attempt to do this with the time that we had, because we were trying to prepare our night defense position, digging in, getting in our resupply and what not. Again, I would estimate the time would be 1530 to 1600 hours. Somewhere between that time, I'm not definite on the time. Sabre – I believe the call sign was Sabre 6 – was the division commander. He was somewhere in vicinity in his helicopter. He broke in on the radio and he said, 'Negative, don't send them back there going through that mess.'"

Capt. Medina stated that Charlie and Bravo Companies were going to ring up for the night together to give each other additional fire power because "we were expecting to make contact with the 48th VC Battalion." These two companies together at that time had reported 128 VC body count. Capt. Medina was overheard in a radio transmission giving a body count of 310. The 48th VC Battalion probably had only 200 men. The question then is what unit, if any, had Task Force Barker been in contact with? Charlie Company had engaged generally only non-combatants and it is felt they were anxious that evening because they expected they might make contact with the 48th VC Battalion, some of whose families most likely had been killed. Of greater interest is why Medina brazenly trumpeted the killing of 310 civilians?

Capt. Medina recalls that both he and Capt. Earl C. Michles received National Police which were brought into their night defensive position. "We then gathered the VC suspects that Michels had and the VC suspects that I had in one group and the National Police were identifying known VC, VC that were a part of the infrastructure. As Earl and I were implacing the companies in defensive positions, I heard two shots. The national police had executed two of the VC. Capt. Michles and I went over and told them to stop this that this was not supposed to be going on."

On the 18th Capt. Medina received a call that Col. Henderson was enroute to his location and for him to secure an LZ for his helicopter. "Col. Henderson came in, in his helicopter. I believe there were three individuals that got out of the helicopter: Col. Henderson, the brigade commander, LTC. Blackledge, the brigade S-2, and I believe there was a LTC Luper who was the commanding officer of the 6/11 Artillery Battalion. The helicopter went back up and Col. Henderson and I moved to an area where we would be covered in case we received any small arms fire. Col. Henderson said that he had received a report from a helicopter pilot that I had killed a woman and that there was a possibility of some atrocities that had been committed in My Lai 4. He asked me if this was true, if I knew anything about it. I told Col. Henderson that, yes, I did shoot a woman and explained the circumstances. He said that he understood, or this was understandable. He asked me if I was aware of any atrocities in My Lai 4. I told him no. He asked me if my people were aware of it, and he asked me if I thought my people could do such a thing, and I told him I did not think American soldiers would do such a thing. He said, 'Okay. We are going to conduct an investigation of this.' Then he called for his helicopter and left. I continued on moving toward the LZ across the causeway." [23]

When Charlie Company was extracted back to LZ Dottie, LTC Barker informed Medina that Col. Henderson had been there to meet the people as they arrived and Henderson queried the troops as to whether they had seen or had committed any atrocities in My Lai 4. According to Medina, Barker said, "Ernest, you have been doing a real fine job. Go on back to the company and just continue doing the good work that you have done…He told me that I should advise the people not to discuss it among themselves or with anybody else. I called the company together to tell them what type of operation it was. I told them that there was an investigation being conducted into the alleged accusations, there were atrocities committed at My Lai 4 and that I myself, as the company commander, was being investigated. I told them that it would be best if they did not discuss it amongst themselves or with anybody else and an investigation would be conducted." Medina's admonishment to his company "not to discuss the operation among themselves or with anybody else" was the most important aspect of the Barker led cover-up of the killing of civilians. If only one soldier had spoken out or had written a congressman, the whole charade would have failed. In fact, Lt. Brooks told Medina that he thought Sgt. Michael Bernhardt was going to write his congressman and Medina called in Bernhardt to advise him "that it would be best that you don't write your congressman…"[28]

The soldiers of Charlie Company remember Capt. Medina's discussion when he called them together to inform them of the investigation.

Specialist Cedrick J. Widmer[29] recalls, "We were to keep it to ourselves and not to discuss it further and that he was going to take the full blame for everything that went on, we were just following his orders."

SP5 Abel Flores[30] felt that Capt. Medina was afraid the enlisted men would talk too much when he stated, "All we heard was that there was an investigation that was coming down. To me, I think he was scared that people were going to talk too much and blow it up and all this stuff. He was trying to tell us to keep quiet, that he'd take care of things." When Flores was asked if it was his impression that this was a cover-up he replied, "Not this. When we got the citation, or they say we got one, I don't know, it was just like a rumor that we were supposed to receive a citation for what we had done. To me that was a cover-up."

Cpl. William H. Kern[31] was aware that something unusual had gone on for when he was asked "Were you aware at this time that a lot of Vietnamese people had been killed", he replied, "Yes, because they said we had a high body count. They said it was three hundred and something."

SP4 Charles Sledge[32] when asked if he remembered what Capt. Medina said was being investigated, stated, "I believe he said that it was being investigated. It was investigated because of the killing of the women and children. I believe he said something about the fact that they were trying to see if he gave orders."

Pfc Dennis M. Bunning[33] had a new twist when he discussed what might happen to someone who wrote home or anything on this kind of stuff, "It was not sage writing home to Congressmen or anybody and they know who write to Congressmen. They'll get back to him and chances of getting knocked off is too easy, because I've had them at least five guys come to me and just plain told me, 'Leave us alone or we'll kill you.'"

Pfc Tommy Moss[34] when asked if anyone besides Capt. Medina told him to keep quiet about what happened that morning at My Lai 4 replied: "No. After that, I guess everybody just forgot all about it, because we didn't hear anything else about it, that much."

A good indication of what went on in the minds of the enlisted personnel in Charlie Company is obtained from Pfc Richard W. Pendleton[35] when he stated: "Well, Capt. Medina said something about there might be an investigation or something. That really surprised us. He said, 'Well, whatever happened I'll stand behind all you people.' That kind of surprised me when he started talking like that. I don't remember about what he said, but I remember that was part of it... I was surprised because right then is when it hit everybody that they did something they weren't supposed to do. I started to think about it right then. Up until then I thought we had done what we were supposed to do. I don't know how all of the men in the company felt. There was some people that felt different I suppose. Some people, I guess some people just didn't really care. Some people that thought, well, they don't want to do this, but they did it anyway, and some people that didn't believe in killing at all. Nobody felt the same about it."

At his meeting Capt. Medina assured the men that they were just following orders and he would take care of things. Most of the men knew that there had been women and children killed and some had heard that the body count was over 300. Undoubtedly, Capt. Medina's admonition not to talk about the My Lai affair was a major factor which kept the information of My Lai 4 from reaching senior authorities. Capt. Medina was a very forceful commander and well-liked by his company soldiers. He had always demanded discipline and his orders were normally closely followed. Not all the men of Charlie Company committed unlawful acts, but for certain they all participated in the cover-up by not discussing the incident.

The First Platoon
The unit swept the southern sector of My Lai 4 committing atrocious acts of cruelty. From the time it entered the hamlet they began the indiscriminate shooting of the non-combatants, and grenades were often thrown into houses killing or maiming the occupants. Just after the insertion a soldier "stabbed a man in the back with his bayonet. The man fell to the ground gasping for breath and the soldier killed him. There were so many killed that day it is hard for me (Stanley) to recall exactly how some of the people died."[109] Platoon members saw 150 to 200 dead bodies consisting mostly of women and children.

Pfc Dennis Conti[36] was a member of the 1st Platoon and he remembers Capt. Medina's briefing as well as an additional one by Lt. Calley, the platoon leader. The mood of the men of the 1st Platoon after the briefing was, "I think we were 'psyched up', ready for battle more or less. But, like I say, we were ready to meet a foe of equal military strength, if not greater. And we prepared to give our best." He recalls that there was a memorial service held just prior to the briefing.

On the day of the operation Conti was carrying a mine sweeper in Lt. Calley's command group. "I was in the first chopper. And I think I found Lt. Calley, and joined up with him. And at the time there was, to the right, along the tree line, a villager with cattle moving out. And I heard somebody yelling, 'They're running away; they're running away. And they opened up with a M-60. I moved up through the village. On the way, I guess, there was a few people killed there, there were bodies there. I moved up, and I met Lt. Calley again in the CP group. When I got there, we were told to round the people up. So myself and (Pfc Paul) Meadlo, I had the mine sweeper and I couldn't do anything, so most of the guys were rounding them up, and bringing them to me and Meadlo. We herded them all together, pushed them out. He said, 'Bring them out into the rice paddy'… They were bringing people out, and then we pushed them out into the rice paddy, onto the dike there. And, like I said, we pushed them out there. Meadlo and myself, we watched them.

While we were watching, a little kid came running out up here, and I went up to investigate. I told him to watch the people. There were women and a baby about 4 years old, who were walking, and an older woman, who I assumed to be a grandmother or something. I rounded them up, brought them back down to Meadlo, and we stood around them for a couple of minutes talking. Lt. Calley came back, and said 'Take care of them.' So we said, 'Okay.' And we sat there and watched them like we usually do. And he came back again, and he said, 'I thought I told you to take care of them.' I said, 'We're taking care of them.' And he said, 'I mean kill them.' So I looked at Meadlo, and he looked at me, and I didn't want to do it. And he didn't want to do it. So we just kept looking at the people, and Calley calls over and says, 'Come here, come here.' People were right around here, where this P-80 is, and we were on the other side. Then he said, 'Come on, we'll line them up here, we'll kill them.' Meadlo willingly publicly discussed his next actions with the CBS network, "He (Lt. Calley) stepped back about 10 to 15 feet, and he started shooting them. And he told me to start shooting. So I started shooting, I poured about four clips into the group. I fired them on automatic—you just spray the area and so you can't know how many you killed 'cause they were going fast."

"We're rounding up more, and we had about seven or eight people. And we was going to throw them in the hooch, and well, we put them in the hooch and then we dropped a hand grenade down there with them. And somebody holed up in the ravine, and told us to bring them over to the ravine, so we took them back out and led them over too—and by that time, we already had them over there, and they had about 70, 75 people, all gathered up. So we threw ours in with them and Lieutenant Calley told me, he said, Meadlo, we got another job to do. And so we walked over to the people, and he started pushing them off and started shooting . . . off into the ravine. It was a ditch. And so we started pushing them off and we started shooting them, so altogether we just pushed them all off, and just started using automatics on them. Men, women, and children. And babies. And so we started shooting them, and somebody told us to switch off to single shot so that we could save ammo. So we switched off to single shot, and shot a few more rounds."[37,38]

After observing the killing of people in the rice paddy, Conti walked up the trail, and wandered back to the village where he saw somebody firing into a ditch. He thought maybe we had been hit, and went over to investigate, to see if anybody needed help. As he walked over to the ditch he observed Lt. Calley and another soldier firing into the ditch which contained women, children, and a couple of old men, just regular civilians. One woman got up, and Calley shot her in the head. She went back down. He didn't feel like watching anymore, and turned around and walked away.

Stanley recalls observing Calley's firing into the ditch "the people in the ditch kept trying to get out and some made it to the top, but before they could get away they were shot too." He also saw an old lady on a bed and there was a priest dressed in white praying over her. Lt. Calley pulled the priest a few feet away from me and shot him with Meadlo's M-16 rifle.[109]

Haeberle's Photo of the Vietnamese Bodies in the Ditch

Peers Inquiry, Vol. 3, Ron Haeberle photograph (b&w)

Conti recalls there would have been forty Vietnamese bodies in the ditch and another forty in the first group that he saw killed. "I would estimate that I saw 150 to 200 dead bodies consisting of women and children. I would say this based upon what I had been able to see so far in the west half of the village."

Conti remembers seeing the helicopter land, "I know a helicopter landed, and a warrant officer was complaining about it. At least that's the word I got, because I was about 150 meters from the helicopter when it landed. I think Lt. Calley and somebody else were over there, and the word came back through the grapevine that he was complaining about the killing or something."

"Like I said, through the grapevine we heard that the warrant officer had gone back and complained to division, and we heard there was an investigation underway. That supposedly – you know, how supposedly everybody was supposed to be going to jail, and Capt. Medina and all the officers were getting hung and we were all going away for 150 years a piece. And then later on we were told that the investigation was dropped, and they told us we had a citation for it, because in the paper it read 128 VC killed."

When asked for his opinion of what really caused the killing of Vietnamese civilians in My Lai 4, Conti summed it up. "I think it was poor leadership on the part of Lt. Calley, for example, his orders at point 4, his attitude toward the men, and their attitude toward him. All these points, plus beforehand we hit a minefield and lost a lot of people. A lot of guys were still shook up and scared from it. Everybody was on edge, just at a psychological point. You could go one way or the other way. And Lt. Calley was a spark for the fire. The orders he gave, and the way he presented himself."

Calley's actions that morning resulted in the cold blooded killing of over 100 innocent civilians. The 1st Platoon which swept the southern sector of My Lai 4 reported overall a minimum of 158 to a maximum of 389 civilian casualties. Additionally some members of the platoon raped women, torched the houses and bayonetted livestock.

Conti's assessment of what really caused the killing is germane. The men were new, scared, on edge and psyched up. They would have gone whichever way their leaders directed them. Unfortunately Lt. Calley sparked the fire which lead to the wanton killing. The grapevine within the company heard that an investigation was underway and the men were going to get rather severe punishments, 150 years a piece. The threat of punishment is probably another causative factor for the participants close-hold of the information concerning the My Lai 4 operation.

The Second Platoon

The unit swept the northern sector of My Lai 4. They also began killing the Vietnamese inhabitants as soon as they entered the village. On several occasions villagers were rounded up in small groups and shot. There were two cases of rape and old men, women and children were killed.

Lt. Stephen Brooks was the platoon leader of the 2nd Platoon. His platoon sergeant was Sfc Jay A. Buchanon. Sgt. Buchanon[39] remembers Capt. Medina's briefing for the entire company on 15 March. They then heard the plans of operation the following day. They were told that there would be a ratio of two enemy for every American soldier. They should arm themselves accordingly. Their mission was to destroy the inhabitants and Sgt. Buchanon thought everyone he would see would be part of the 48th VC Battalion. The first and second platoons were to sweep the village of My Lai and the third platoon had the mission of burning the village. Since some villages had been burned previously by Task Force Barker, he did not feel it was unusual for the third platoon to have that mission.

The second platoon went in on the second lift into My Lai 4 area on 16 March. Sgt. Buchanon stated that he ran across the open field and that the troops from the other lift had already gone into the village. His platoon was on the left (north) side of the village. When he landed he heard a tremendous amount of fire in the village but he didn't take any fire that day nor were there any casualties in his platoon that day.

1Sgt. Buchanon said his platoon went into the north edge of My Lai 4 and then into a sub-hamlet. Lt. Brooks wanted the sub-hamlet, Binh Tay, located about one hundred meters north of My Lai 4, searched and so we went across an open field in three columns into the sub-hamlet. Once in the hamlet Sgt. Buchanon went along a path and saw a doorway. He went into this doorway and it led into a prepared tunnel. After going some way into the tunnel he found some suitcases with pajamas and documents. At that time he heard some firing and he ran out of the tunnel in the direction toward the sound of firing. He saw five to ten dead bodies of men and women lying close together. Lt. Brooks arrived about the same time and asked what happened and everyone said they didn't know anything about it. Lt. Brooks was angry. Sgt. Buchanon knew that the bodies were not there when his platoon went into the village so they had been recently shot. He couldn't tell how they were killed but assumed it was by small arms fire. He didn't see any weapons or web gear on this group.

After that killing the platoon went back into the village and rounded up everybody. Later the people were released. At that time Sgt. Buchanon saw the rest of the company leaving the village for the night defensive position, so his platoon joined the rest of the company. That day Sgt. Buchanon did not give a body count and Lt. Brooks did not ask for one.

The 2nd Platoon which swept the northern half of My Lai 4 reported a minimum of seventeen to a maximum of twenty-seven civilian casualties. Women were raped, houses burned and property laid waste.

The Third Platoon
The unit under Lt. Jeffrey V. La Cross was in the second airlift and landed at 7:47am. They were to follow the other platoons with orders to burn the village. They were accompanied by the weapons platoon.

Sp4 Kinch[22] was an 81mm mortarman assigned to the weapons platoon. He too remembers Capt. Medina's briefing. It was his understanding that the company was going in there to destroy the village and everything within the area including humans. Sp4 Kinch went on the last – second lift. When he got on the ground his group set up the mortar tube and waited for word to fire or break down. Most of the troops were in the village. He heard the steady sound of fire. He can distinguish an American weapon from a Vietnamese weapon and there were no Vietnamese weapons fired. They moved out. After a call from Capt. Medina they moved southwest until they made a turn at the outskirts of the village when they received a call that a man had been wounded. They sat down and waited for the medivac helicopter to come. At that time Sp4 Kinch saw a boy between four and eight years old running from south to north and an automatic weapon open up and the boy fell to the ground. He got up and began running again and the weapon opened up again. This time the boy fell but did not get up. There were bodies all over the path but he didn't see how the bodies other than the boy's got there. When shown a photograph he recognized the boy in the picture and drew an arrow to indicate which body he thought was the boy's. The boy was easy to identify because he had a red shirt on. About that time Capt. Medina received a call from someone saying that the medevac said there were bodies all over the place and wanted to know why. Capt. Medina said that he did not know but would find out. Sp4 Kinch said Capt. Medina called forward on the radio and said, "That's enough shooting for the day. The party's over." The firing died down and they went through the village.

The village was on fire at the time. Sp4 Kinch saw the bodies an old man and a young girl and a small infant all near a house. Capt. Medina told Sgt.

Maroney to burn the hooches that were not already burning and Sp4 Kinch saw a couple of men in his platoon set fire to the houses with cigarette lighters. About 80 percent of the portion of the village he was in was already burning. Sp4 Kinch said they then came upon a ditch with forty or fifty bodies of women and children. There were other bodies scattered throughout the area, from twenty to sixty women and children. I didn't see any weapons in the village and he didn't take any fire that day.

Haeberle's Photo of Burning Houses

Peers Inquiry, Vol. 3, Ron Haeberle photograph (b&w)

After they left the village they went east and stopped for lunch just outside the village where they ate and waited for a booby trap to be blown up. The Charlie Company platoon leaders gathered about Capt. Medina during lunch.

Sp4 Kinch stated he was in a daze because he did not believe 'what he had seen.' The command group went east for the rest of the day and as they were walking along the path somebody called for a body count and Capt. Medina said "310". Sp4 Kinch said he could remember because he was shocked by the figure at the time. They continued east until they came to their night position.

Sgt. Martin E. Fagan[40] was also with the 81mm mortar platoon. He says their mission was to move into the village and burn hooches, chop down trees, and shoot cows and chickens. Sgt. Fagan stated that he saw about 100 to 150 bodies that day. He didn't see a ditch with a large number of bodies in it. Of the bodies he saw there were mostly women and children and elderly men. There were some males between eight and fifteen years old and he would consider them to be of military age.

Sgt. Fagan was shocked about the incident and then indifferent. He saw a sizable group of about fifteen to twenty-five people close together next to a trail with a fence behind them. It looked like they were killed by small arms fire. He didn't think the people he saw that day were killed by artillery. Fagan says that on two occasions Capt. Medina on the radio asked to have his mission changed from search and destroy to search and clear.

Kinch's visual observations coupled with Haeberle's pictures indicate that the majority of the houses in the village were set on fire by ground troops in compliance with Capt. Medina's orders. All of Charlie Company was involved in the needless killing of non-combatants, which in the total area amounted to a minimum of 175 to a maximum of 416 civilian casualties with a best estimate of 408 killed.

What could have caused this outstanding unit recently transferred from Hawaii to have so completely lost its composure, seriously violating the Laws of War? A review of events leading up to the assault provides insights into the situation.

On 26 January 1968 Charlie Company relocated to LZ Dottie in the Batangan Peninsula to provide security. On 1 February 1968 Charlie Company was ordered to patrol the countryside searching for the enemy which after the Tet attacks had supposedly withdrawn into the area. Days upon days of fruitless looking for an enemy the company could not distinguish from the local villagers created a sense of disillusionment and a feeling of contempt towards the Vietnamese. Commencing in mid-February the company was involved in a series of incidents that resulted in a large number of casualties. The troops became frustrated and angry and began to manhandle the natives. As casualties increased there was a breakdown of discipline and the gravity of the offenses escalated to include rape and murder. When the perpetrators were not punished many soldiers believed those acts were to be condoned. By 15 March Charlie Company had incurred a total of twenty-four casualties including six killed.

About mid-March LTC Barker developed a plan to find and eliminate the 48th VC Force and to eradicate its home base, believed to be My Lai 4. He directed Charlie Company under Capt. Medina, a highly competitive officer desiring to prove himself, to lead the assault. The evening prior to the attack Capt. Medina called his company together to outline his concept of the operation and to motivate his troops. The following morning during the assault on My Lai 4 in a period of four hours; numerous women, children and old men were brutally assaulted and killed, primarily by Charlie Company soldiers. Thankfully, a large number of Charlie Company soldiers on the operation did not participate in the killings at My Lai 4; however the mindset of those who did participate can be determined by the fact that many considered it a charitable act to shoot and kill wounded villagers in order to put them out of their misery.

Why? Many infantry units in Vietnam had situations similar to the one Charlie Company encountered. Others had taken serious casualties from the ubiquitous mines and booby traps; they had endured countless days and nights on the difficult terrain searching for an elusive enemy; they, too, had difficulty differentiating the enemy from the local population; and they had known disillusionment, frustration and anger. What then could be the reason that Charlie Company so blatantly violated the Laws of War by indiscriminating killing non-combatants? It can be surmised that the key factor explaining Charlie Company's actions was most likely Capt. Medina's highly motivational company briefing the evening just prior to the attack.

This outstanding highly respected officer called Charlie Company together the evening before the scheduled operation to brief them on his plan of attack and to motivate his men. For its psychological impact, he purposely chose the time of the briefing to immediately follow the memorial service for a very popular company NCO who had been killed the day before by an enemy booby trap. His efforts to psyche-up his inexperienced troops exceeded beyond his expectations. Almost all the soldiers interrogated concerning My Lai 4 brought up the subject of Medina's briefing. Medina told his men they were going to meet a very tough enemy that would out number them two to one. He instructed them to kill all the livestock and to burn down the hamlet. Nothing was to be left alive but themselves. He said that any Vietnamese left in the hamlet would be VC or VC sympathizers and mentioned that this was the company's chance to get even. So the next morning this psyched up, frustrated, angry, scared and highly motivated group of young men started out on their first combat assault during which many of the soldiers believed they were following orders when they randomly killed the inhabitants of My Lai 4. Charlie Company's previously unpunished breaches of conduct (burning of houses, rape, murder) exploded in scope on the 16 March 1968 operation as these frustrated soldiers sought revenge for hurts received from unknown Vietnamese.

The 31st Public Information Detachment

Lt. John W. Moody[41] was the commanding officer of the detachment which was assigned to the 11th Brigade. Just prior to 16 March operation Col. Henderson established the policy that all combat assaults would be covered by the detachment. He[41] stated that Spc. Ronald L. Haeberle volunteered for the assignment because he was getting short and Spc. Jay Roberts was assigned as a writer to accompany him because the two had good rapport. The reports submitted by Haeberle and Roberts that day were very influential because they supported LTC Barker's on-going cover-up efforts.

Spc. Haeberle[42] remembers that he took three cameras with him the day of the operation. Two of them were Army cameras with black and white film and one was his own personal camera with color film. He and Spc. Roberts were assigned to a helicopter in the second lift and after landing in the LZ they were grouped with the third platoon of Charlie Company which was headed toward Highway 521.

On the way down to Highway 521 Spc. Haeberle recalls that he saw a woman shot from behind the hedgerow. A GI just kept firing at her until the bones were flying. There were about three to fifteen soldiers firing at this woman as though it was target practice. On the way toward Highway 521 the soldiers fired in the general direction of women and children walking along the trail and it looked like they were hit. Spc. Haeberle is certain that none of the troops he accompanied that day received any fire from anyone.

Spc. Haeberle recalls seeing a man and two small children about four and five years old walking towards the troops, coming down from the gully behind the road. The man looked like he could be of military age. Spc. Haeberle saw these people killed. He remembers there were two small boys, one about four years old and the other seven or eight years old. These boys seemed to come from nowhere. The soldiers fired upon them and a tracer round hit the younger boy in the chest and seemed to burn there. The older one jumped on the younger one and in the picture of the boys are still alive or at least Spc. Haeberle thought the older one was still alive, and they were shot thereafter. This incident occurred as the troops were moving back towards the south of My Lai to the area where a pilot had dropped a smoke grenade on the North-South trail. As they were walking toward the village, he noticed a group of fifty plus people about

100 yards from him. They were women and children. Women with babies were squatting and several GI's were in front of them. Some of the GI's were walking off and he heard firing. It looked as if a machine gunner with an ammo bearer were just spraying the group with bullets. Later Spc. Haeberle looked for the pile of bodies. It was not yet 9 o'clock.

When Spc. Haeberle's group arrived at the village there was mass confusion. Spc. Haeberle observed a dead woman in bed who appeared to be shot. One photo shows a burning building with three bodies lying outside of it – a man – a woman – and a baby. He remembers a GI who went berserk running around stabbing a calf with his bayonet. The soldier seemed to be getting a kick out of the stabbing.

One photograph was of people just before they were shot. GI's were standing around the people and one GI was trying to take the blouse off the one girl and when he saw Spc. Haeberle taking the picture he quit. Jay Roberts and Haeberle started to walk away and heard firing. They looked back and saw the bodies falling. Spc. Haeberle was only five to six yards away and the M-16's of the GI's were still smoking.

In the area where he took photos Haeberle saw a boy about eight or nine years old and crouched down to take the picture. As he was still looking through the lens a GI to his left shot the boy. The first shot moved the boy back, a second lifted him off the ground and the third caused him to flip over. The boy fell and the body fluids came out. About the same time a very small boy who only had a shirt on came into the area and put his hands on one of the boys. He looked like he was looking for his mother. A soldier shot him and he just flipped up and landed on top of the boys.

When asked what the general talk amongst the troops was during the operation, Haeberle said, "Well, we had to." When Spc.'s Haeberle and Roberts went back to Duc Pho they decided not to say anything about the operation unless asked. They didn't talk about the operation in the office.

Lt. Moody states that he could tell that Spc.'s Haeberle and Roberts were upset and distressed about the operation but he thought it was because they had seen some casualties. Lt. Moody said a lot of people took color slides themselves but when he went through the photographs available before this investigation he could only conclude that Spc. Haeberle exercised considerable editorial judgment in taking the color pictures. The disparity between the content on the black and white and color photos is major. The black and white official photographs are bland in content whereas the personal color photos show atrocities. Lt. Moody felt that Spc. Haeberle thought he had a gold mine in the photographs and was going to use them. Lt. Moody believes that Spc. Haeberle even during the combat assault was trying to suppress information to use at a later time for his own benefit.

Spc. Haeberle looked through the color pictures which he had taken that day of the wanton killing of women and children and said that the photos were a fair and accurate representation of what he saw on 16 March 1968. The pictures provide a graphic visual portrayal of the results of the operation. He captured the slaughter, the burning of the village, and the tedium of the soldiers most vividly. His oral description of the murder of a young boy epitomizes the pathos and his color photos are proof positive of the extent of the non-combatant killings.

Spc. Roberts wrote a very positive and fictitious news article about the Task Force Barker operation that was published in the Americal Division newspaper, Trident. It described contacts throughout the morning and early afternoon which resulted in 128 enemy killed. Also as the soldiers moved through the marshes a mile west of My Lai they spotted sixty-nine enemy bodies killed by ground troops and a battery of the 6/11 Artillery Battalion. There was no mention of civilian casualties or any of the atrocities he had observed. Subsequent to the Trident story the Stars and Stripes also picked up and published the laudatory results of the operation where 128 VC were killed. Thus Robert's false account of the My Lai 4 operation was well publicized.

Both Haeberle and Roberts witnessed the hamlet's destruction and the killings, yet for unknown reasons they both decided to falsify their reports. Haeberle by submitting bland black and white official photos that failed to depict any of the carnage, while keeping for himself vivid color photos of the massacre. Roberts deliberately falsified his written report that described a contested battle with 128 enemy killed, thereby supporting Barker's and Medina's accounting of the incident.

Bravo Company 4th Battalion/3rd Infantry
The Task Force Barker operation against My Lai 4 on 16 March 1968 included all three companies in the task force. Charlie Company 1st/20th Infantry was the lead assault unit. Bravo Company 4th/3rd Infantry was to intercept the enemy evading Charlie Companies actions. Alpha Company 1st/3rd Infantry was to assume a blocking position well to the north of My Lai 4. Mr. Ridenhour's letter mentioned only the actions of Charlie Company and the initial investigations focused only on that unit. Well into its investigation the Peers Inquiry determined that Bravo Company may

have committed crimes and it expanded its scope to include it. Alpha Company was not involved in violations.

Capt. Earl C. Michles was the commander of Bravo Company which was an integral part of the Task Force Barker. It air assaulted into a landing zone south of My Lai 4 at 0815 hours with the task of intercepting any of the 48th VC Local Force Battalion attempting to withdraw from My Lai 4 as a result of Charlie Company's attack. Subsequently it was to move northward, search My Lai (1) and rendezvous with Charlie Company in a night bivouac. The 1st Platoon under Lt. Thomas K. Willingham after landing moved north to highway 521 and then crossed over a bridge to a barrier spit of land where at the hamlets of My Khe (4) and Co Lay (1) they received sniper fire. Responding, the 1st Platoon, which consisted of two squads totaling twenty-two troops, reported killing 38 VC. The Son Tinh District chief alleged that 90 civilians in Co Lay (1) hamlet had been killed. The 2nd Platoon moving northward almost immediately hit a land mine and the platoon leader was killed and 4 soldiers wounded. After reorganizing the platoon moved out again and within 100 yards detonated another land mine wounding an additional three men. The morale of the company was seriously affected with these causalities and the company continued to move towards its rendezvous night location with Charlie Company.

After the Peers Inquiry broadened its investigation to include the actions of Bravo Company 4th/3rd Infantry it determined that indiscriminate killing had occurred during the operation by the 1st Platoon. Task Force Barker combined the thirty-eight VC casualties reported by Bravo Company with the ninety VC killed by Charlie Company and reported a total 128 VC body count.

Artillery Support
LTC Barker and Capt. Medina both claimed that the civilian casualties at My Lai 4 were caused by artillery and gunship firings and not by ground troops. A review of the artillery and gunship support is essential to determine if that was true.

Lt. Col. Robert V. Luper[43] the commanding officer of the 6th Battalion, 11th Artillery, recalled that the artillery support of the 16th March operation was provided by D Battery, a provisional unit located at LZ Uptight. The battery was efficient by mid-March but not as efficient as the other batteries. He stated that the battery commander, Capt. Steven J. Gamble and the artillery liaison officer, Capt. Vasquez, would at all times know what was going on with respect to artillery support at Task Force Barker. Artillery clearance would have been through Capt. Vasquez to the Son Tinh

District where there was a NCO stationed with the advisory team to facilitate clearances. Usually, clearance was given immediately upon request, for any place within this particular area.

Luper remembers hearing about sixty-nine VC killed by artillery sometime in the morning of the 16th, "I do not know that any innocent civilians or non-combatants were killed by artillery. I still do not know it to this day. When somebody said there might have been civilians killed by artillery or gunships, I felt no obligation to report this as an artillery incident." He said sixty-nine would be a very large number of KIA's to be attributed to artillery in Vietnam. As an artillery commander he never had an occasion to turn in body count.[44]

Capt. Steven J. Gamble[45] was commanding officer of D Battery, 6th Battalion, 11th Artillery, since February 1968. He had four tubes of 105mm. He remembers telling Col. Mason J. Young, the Divarty Commander, one month later on a command visit to LZ Uptight, that his battery had been credited along with air strikes as having a body count of sixty-nine. "When I mentioned this, LTC Luper, to the best of my recollection, said, 'We're not sure that those were all enemy.' That was all that was mentioned to me at the time while I was in country." Capt. Gamble stated that even if civilians were wounded a formal investigation would be required.

Capt. Vasquez[18] stated the prep was the only artillery fired into the My Lai 4 area on 16 March 1968. While in Vietnam no one ever questioned him about the My Lai 4 operation. He stated that if he were aware of non-combatants being killed by artillery fire in the operation he would have communicated to the battery commander. He was not aware of non-combatants killed as result of artillery fire at My Lai 4 on 16 March 1968. He recalls being given a body count of sixty-nine about one-half hour after the assault. He didn't see any bodies in the LZ area.

Lt. Roger L. Alaux was the artillery forward observer with Charlie Company. He had the impression that orders to destroy the village of My Lai 4 came from higher up because "This was one of the few operations that we had, where we had as many National Police present as we did on the particular operation." When asked if he thought ARVN wanted this place wiped out, he said, "I know they did. It has been a thorn in their side for 15 years." Lt. Alaux states that his radio operator (RTO) got an ammo count of ninety-nine rounds for the entire prep, which was not out of the question and very possible. He thought that the artillery prep got into the village to a good extent. Alaux stated, "Nobody called me for artillery support. I was just waiting to do my job. And as far as the number sixty-nine I really don't know where that came from … This is a number – well, it didn't come from me because I didn't make a count. It didn't come from me. I accepted that number." [46]

LTC Luper, Capt. Gamble, Capt. Vasquez and Lt. Alaux were all aware of the report that sixty-nine VC were killed by artillery that day at My Lai 4. When the location of the preparatory fires is compared with the reported location of Vietnamese personnel killed as result of combat operations there is no correlation. Therefore, it is assumed that very few, if any, non-combatants were killed at My Lai 4 as result of the artillery preparatory fires. Nevertheless, when LTC Barker reported civilians killed by artillery, LTC Luper should have initiated an artillery investigation. LTC Luper's total indifference to the results of the artillery prep that day is perplexing. Had he checked into the artillery situation or initiated an artillery investigation it would have been obvious that the reporting of Task Force Barker was undeniably false. No effort at all was made by the artillery personnel, or by Col. Henderson either, to justify the bogus report of sixty-nine VC killed by artillery. The reports of VC killed, were just a numbers game played by LTC Barker and Capt. Medina. There was no battle. They killed no enemy. The report of sixty-nine killed by artillery in an open field one mile west of My Lai 4 was ludicrous and should have been a red flag to any discerning reviewer of the report.

Aviation Support
The army aviation involvement in the combat assault was provided by the gunships and troop carrying capabilities of the 174th Aviation Company and the reconnaissance activities of the aero scouts of the 123rd Aviation Battalion. The 174th Aviation Company had only one gun team on station on the morning of 16 March. Statements of both pilots indicate that they probably made two suppressing runs along the sides of the LZ. LTC Barker gave the doorgunners on troop carrying helicopters permission to shoot as required. Both Capt. McCrary and WO Doersam had little of significance to report concerning the suppressing fires. They remember only two incidents where the 174th (Sharks) engaged VC. One was to the south of the village after the first lift had landed where Capt. McCrary found a VC with weapon. The second was north of the village where they engaged two VC with weapons, web gear and in uniforms and killed them out in the open. He doesn't believe his trail ship engaged anyone.

Capt. Lanny J. McCrary[47] was a gunship platoon leader and was flying the lead gunship on 16 March 1968. The gunships had two systems to suppress, the mini-guns and a 40mm grenade launcher. He recalls South of Highway 521 there was "a regular Vietnamese tree line with the trees about every four feet, right along here. Now here on the trail, we saw about three or four, five, half a dozen people killed … by ground troops. We were just right in this area, circling about 150 or 200 feet. Like I say, I observed some people that were killed, because it was unusual and we mentioned it to each other, like, 'What's going on,' or 'What's the matter,' you know, 'What's the deal there.' As one man got through the tree line to the south, and it was a little bit east of where – we were in this area and this is where the man was. I assumed that it was Charlie 6, because the RTO was right behind him, right in the tree line and just south of the tree line where we observed a woman killed. Because I remember mentioning it to -- it was mentioned in the aircraft, 'Look that guy just shot a woman.'"

McCrary remembers the division commander on the radio stating, "What's going on down there?" … "I remember mentioning that Big 6 was there and made some remark as to what's going on down there, because he just never talked on the radio. I believe Mr. Doersam over VHF possibly said something to me to the effect like, 'You know, something's going on down there that shouldn't be going on,' and things like this, or a whole lot of people being killed or something to the effect or something like this." McCrary relates that he saw approximately 50 bodies scattered throughout the area along Highway 521 and he actually saw three to six people killed by ground troops in this area. In addition, he saw what he thought was Charlie 6 kill a woman.

Warrant Office Russell E. Doersam,[48] a gunship pilot, believes that both gunships prepped along the edge of the village. He remembers killing the two VC wearing blue ascots in the rice paddy with weapons and packs. His recollection was almost identical to Capt. McCrary when asked if he or Shark Lead made any gun runs or firing passes, Mr. Doersam replied, "Outside the prep there were none. No rockets fired or mini-gun fire. I didn't see anybody besides ourselves and the Warlords in that one incident, engaging anyone." He remembers seeing thirty or forty bodies in a ditch at the eastern edge of the village. "It looked like they were herded in and machine-gunned down…they were just lying down in one big mass there." When asked if he were questioned specifically by anyone, he relied "No, I wasn't."

Warrant Officer Hugh C. Thompson Jr.[49], of the 123rd Aviation Battalion, the pilot of the observation helicopter, was the key man in the aero scout team which supported Charlie Company on their combat assault. This was his first combat assault. He had working with him on his scout team two gunships, a low gunship which flew at an elevation approximately 800 to 1000 feet and a high gunship which operated at an altitude of 1200 to 1500 feet. The OH-23 had communications with the low gunship and the high gunship had communications with the Bravo Company TOC and normally with the ground unit being supported. The OH-23 had very limited radio control. He arrived on station at My Lai at approximately 0730 hours, just about the time the "slicks" were touching down. He saw a VC with a weapon and his crew opened up on it.

He maneuvered to stop two VC suspects that were among a substantial number of Vietnamese on Highway 521 moving toward Quang Ngai City and remembers firing in front of these people to detain them. The two suspects were picked up by Col. Henderson and flown to LZ Dottie. He did not see gunships fire on the Vietnamese on the road nor did he see ground troops fire on the people on Highway 521. WO Thompson fired his weapons only twice on March 16th.

Thompson said he saw one girl in a rice paddy and one wounded woman on the road moving her arms. There were several more wounded people in the fields. He called his low gunship to tell of the wounded and he believes he requested a dust-off. He does not think the dust-off was available so he popped smoke hoping to call the attention of the ground troops to the wounded. He did not have communications with the ground troops and received his messages through the low gunship and the high gunship usually had radio contact with the ground troops. After he popped smoke he hovered over the wounded and some friendlies started moving south. WO Thompson saw a Captain go over to a wounded woman and nudge her. The Captain then turned back and fired at the woman. WO Thompson, who was observing from an elevation of 25 feet and about 50 yards away, did not understand why the woman was killed.

WO Thompson said they couldn't fly over the western half of the village because the smoke was too thick. The western part of the village was apparently burned, so he moved over to the eastern end of the village where there was a ditch 100 to 200 yards long and 10 feet wide. There he observed fifty to a hundred dead and wounded bodies in the ditch. There were females, children, babies and old men bunched close together. WO Thompson said he set his chopper down about twenty-five yards from the ditch and motioned for the friendlies to come over. He talked to a colored NCO and asked if the NCO could help the wounded in the ditch, who replied, "The only way he could help them was to put them out of their misery."

They just kept reconning some more and the next thing he recalls was when the crew saw some women and kids in a bunker doorway. There was a horseshoe area near the bunker and he saw some US soldiers approaching the bunker. He feared for the safety of the Vietnamese and so he landed on the ground. He was approached by Lt. Calley and he made an expression to his crew to fire at the American soldiers if they open fire on the people at the bunker. WO Thompson asked Lt. Calley if he could get the Vietnamese out of the bunker and LT. Calley said only way he knew to get them out was with a hand grenade. WO Thompson told the infantrymen to hold where they were and he called on one of his teams' gunships to come down and lift the people out. WO Millians made two trips to get the Vietnamese out of the bunker.

Subsequently, WO Thompson landed his aircraft again near the ditch and the crew spotted some people moving. The crew chief and gunner went to the ditch and brought back a child. The live baby that they had spotted on the other trip over the ditch was now dead and was missing part of its head. They took the Vietnamese child to the hospital at Quang Ngai and returned back to LZ Dottie.

Thompson felt that he had seen a minimum of seventy-five bodies and maximum of 150 bodies around the village. The majority of the bodies were women and children and there were no weapons or web gear on the bodies.

Maj. Frederick W. J. Watke, Commanding Officer, Company B, (Aero-Scout), 123rd Aviation Battalion flew low gunship on the first support mission and he came on station in time to see all the artillery prep, some of which went into the LZ area and a few into the village. "We stayed to the south. We never did go up over the troops initially because the decision was made shortly after the first lift, when the LZ was not hot, and the troops were able to reorganize and handle themselves. The decision was made to go with the second lift as planned into the second LZ. I went off station after the second lift. Our fuel was running low and I pulled off station and I reported that I felt that continuation of our mission down here was rather futile.[50]

Warrant Officer Jerry O. Culverhouse was assigned as a warrant officer gunner on a Huey-B assigned to Bravo Company, 123rd Aviation Battalion. He flew on the 16 March operation as co-pilot gunner in support of the ground force unit. He arrived on station at about 0930 hours. Prior to flying over the village of My Lai 4 he noticed that it was on fire. Most of the fire and flames were coming from the eastern portions of the village. About fifty percent by his estimate was burning. He saw bodies throughout the village and in the rice paddies. South of the village on a dirt road he saw fifteen to twenty bodies in one grouping and another eight to ten bodies to the west of the village. He identified a grouping with men, women and children. He also observed bodies to the east of the village in the southern portion of a ditch about six to eight feet wide and 200 feet long.[51] The bodies in the ditch were men, women and children dressed in normal Vietnamese attire and heaped from one side to another for about twenty-five to thirty feet. I think there were about fifty to seventy-five people in the ditch. There was water in the ditch and much blood in the water.

About an hour after he arrived on station he saw some people hiding in a bunker and they were spotted by WO Thompson who said he was going to land his helicopter and take them into custody. WO Thompson landed and WO Culverhouse circled the OH-23 to protect it. Finally Thompson made a radio transmission to Culverhouse which stated he wanted the Huey to land and help to evacuate these non-combatant civilians. The Huey questioned Thompson's decision who stated he had asked someone on the ground to take the Vietnamese in custody and they said that they could not. Therefore, WO Thompson felt he must do it himself. WO Culverhouse believes that if we didn't take these people out they would have been killed. The Huey sat down and took out ten to twelve Vietnamese in two trips.

WO Culverhouse estimated the number of bodies on the ground in the entire area at about 175 to 200 bodies. Of these seventy-five percent were women and children. He says he never saw an exchange of fire that day.

Warrant Officer Charles H. Mansell remembers that he flew in a UH-1B that day as cover for the OH-23 scout. His flight record shows that he spent about 4 hours in and around My Lai 4. He escorted WO Thompson to the hospital at Quang Ngai. He doesn't know how he learned about it but he feels sure that he knew at the time that WO Thompson was taking a child to the hospital. "I recall seeing dead bodies along a road that ran east and west south of the village and would say there were twenty to twenty-five bodies. I also saw dead bodies in-around the village. Some of the bodies were groups and singly, I would say the largest group was three to four persons." WO Mansell said he did not fire his gunship at all that day. He was never questioned by his superiors concerning the incident at My Lai 4.[52]

WO Mansell had an occasion to fly over My Lai 4 at a later date. "Yes. I believe it was the next day when I flew over the area. I observed a large amount of dead bodies lying about. It appeared to me that none of them had been moved."

LTC John L. Holladay, Commanding Officer of the 123rd Aviation Battalion, stated[65] that Col. Henderson had operational control of the Aero Scouts. After Col. Henderson's order to resweep the village with the ground troops of Charlie Company had been countermanded by General Koster, it would have been possible for Col. Henderson, either on the afternoon of the 16th or on the morning of the 17th of March, to have ordered an aerial reconnaissance to determine the number of apparent non-combatant casualties as well as the location of these casualties. Such a mission, because the Aero Scouts flew out of LZ Dottie, probably would not have taken more than one hour from its conception to its execution.

It appears that neither the aircraft of the 174th Aviation Company nor those of Bravo Company, 123rd Aviation Battalion did much firing in the vicinity of My Lai 4 in support of the ground troops. Only four or five occasions can be recalled by ground personnel or aviators and the results of each of these engagements with one exception produced tangible evidence of positive identification, that is, VC killed with weapons or web gear or two suspects picked up. Therefore, it can be concluded that few non-combatant casualties, if any, were the result of indiscriminate firing by helicopters.

Without exception the testimony of every aviator indicates that he saw many non-combatant casualties in the vicinity of My Lai 4 on 16 March. They also observed a large amount of smoke emanating from My Lai 4 caused by burning houses.

In this sorry episode at My Lai 4 the only heroic actions were those taken by WO Thompson and his 123rd Aviation Battalion associates who bravely protected and carried to safety in their helicopter a group of threatened Vietnamese non-combatants, transported a wounded child to a Vietnamese hospital and forthrightly reported to their superiors that they had observed many dead non-combatants during the operation.

Brigade Oversight
Col. Henderson remembers that those accompanying him on 16 March in the 11th Brigade Command and Control chopper were: Capt. Cooney, as pilot with a co-pilot and two door-gunners; Maj. McKnight in the left jump seat; CSM Walsh in the right jump seat; himself seated next to the left door; Sgt. Adcock seated next to him; LTC MacLachlan and LTC Luper seated on the right hand side of the aircraft; however, the seat next to the right hand door was unoccupied.

Col. Henderson supervisory activities on 16 March are discussed. His aircraft had mechanical troubles at Duc Pho and took off late, arriving in the area of the combat assault twenty to twenty-five minutes after the artillery prep commenced, that is, about 0750 hours. The first thing Col. Henderson can recall was that the gunships had killed a couple of VC with weapons and that these gunships were having difficulty getting troops over to police up the weapons. He had the C&C fly over to look over the bodies and circled the area for ten to fifteen minutes until he was assured that there were some troops coming toward the bodies from the north of My Lai 4 to pick up the weapons, thereby wasting valuable observation time to recover VC weapons.[17]

At the junction of the trail coming out of My Lai 4 and Highway 521, someone in his aircraft spotted what appeared to be military equipment and the aircraft made low orbits over the area and the pilot attempted to set the craft down near the three or four bodies at this location, but couldn't land because of the terrain. Again, ten to fifteen minutes of valuable supervisory time were spent to police a few dead bodies.

Although Col. Henderson's memory is spotty concerning the time sequence, he feels that he next flew over to see the combat assault of Bravo Company. According to the Task Force Barker log the first Bravo Company combat assault occurred at 0815 hours and the second lift was completed 0827 hours. When he returned to the area of My Lai 4 "I noticed the large number of civilians that were moving along Highway 521 to the west toward Quang Ngai City." Before he picked up the suspects in this group of civilians and took them to LZ Dottie, he had one conversation with Barker regarding a house he had just seen burst into flames, he had already seen three or four houses burning, and here is a fourth one or a fifth one.[17] Although Col Henderson saw no gunships he thought that the hooches were burning as result of gunship fire. "I have only assumed that in the prep – I feel that I have assumed this from the fact that there was an artillery prep and a gunship prep." Col. Henderson did not know how much artillery was fired. "I know now, that it is fact – reasonable fact that no other artillery was fired during this three day operation. I did not know this, or would not have guessed this previously."

When asked what radio he monitored while flying in his C&C, Col. Henderson stated, "I kept one radio on the brigade command net ... I tried to monitor the active nets ... I had two radio frequencies off of the console, FM freqs., and those were my capability."

After dropping off the VC suspects at LZ Dottie, sometime about 0830 hours, Col. Henderson returned to the immediate vicinity of My Lai 4. When informed that General Koster was going to be at LZ Dottie, Col.

Henderson states that he returned to LZ Dottie where he met MG Koster at 0935 hours at the helipad. When questioned about what he was doing as he observed the combat assault that morning up until about 0915 to 0930 hours, Col. Henderson replied, "I would be monitoring a great amount. At the same time, this was my first combat assault and I feel that I had extensive intercom communications with, especially, Maj. McKnight. I also feel that I would have had them with other people aboard the aircraft, although I have heard them testify in which none of them had a headset. This seems strange to me at this time because I didn't know too damn much about a combat assault operation up until this point in time."

"When I observed immediately to the south of My Lai 4 some bodies there, I am also associating this with having called Barker and asked how this happened and I am saying that Col. Barker said that it was probably the result of artillery fire ... And when this was reported to me by Col. Barker that this was the cause of these casualties, by artillery fire, that is the conversation overheard by Luper and is what caused Luper to disclaim responsibility of his artillery. I can see LTC Luper sitting in that aircraft and saying something to the effect 'By God, I'm sick and tired of being accused of -- my artillery being accused of fouling up up here in this area', or something to that effect." [17]

With respect to the number of bodies he saw that day, Col. Henderson stated, "I saw those two, I saw the three or four that were at the junction of Highway 521 and the North-South trail coming out of My Lai 4; I saw the three or four that were to the north of that location on the North-South trail halfway between My Lai 4 and Highway 521. And those were the only bodies that I saw in, around, from there out to the coast." Col. Henderson has always believed that the group of non-combatants he saw half way down the North-South trail towards Highway 521 could not have been killed by small arms, but had been killed by either artillery or gunship firings. This belief had an important impact on his investigative efforts. He did not overfly Highway 521 until approximately 0830. Therefore, either US troops had been in the area or US troops were in the area when Col. Henderson arrived to the south of My Lai 4 and saw the dead non-combatants on the North-South trail. A proper investigation would have indicated this to him. The Vietnamese along the trails definitely were killed by small arms prior to Col. Henderson's over-flight of the area south of My Lai 4 as observed by Capt. McCrary, pilot of a gunship of 174th Aviation Company, who stated that south of Highway 521 there was "a regular Vietnamese tree line with the trees about every 4 feet, right along here. Now here on the trail we saw about three or four, five, half a dozen people killed... by ground troops. We were just right in this area, circling about 150 or 200 feet."

Col. Henderson conducted several conversations with LTC Barker that morning. One was to tell Col. Barker to stop the burning. Another was regarding the process of forwarding combat reports from Task Force Barker to the 11th Brigade and it is possible that a third was a direction to stop the unnecessary killing.

At LZ Dottie Col. Henderson discussed the VC suspects who in actuality turned out to be Vietnamese Popular Forces personnel and he told MG Koster about having observed six to eight bodies, some of which might have been civilians. "It seems to me that at the time that this conversation came out that I was describing to him of having picked up these VC's and that I had called over an OH-23 and that they had placed on some fire alongside this civilian – this group of civilians that were evacuating the area, and he said 'Have you got any reports of any civilians being injured' and I informed him 'No, I don't have any reports from Col. Barker of any civilians being injured up to this point. However, I personally observed six to eight bodies in the area, some of which might be civilians.' And his instructions to me were, 'Well I hope no other --- let's don't get anybody hurt. Ask Barker to give you a report and relay it to me.'" Col. Henderson believes that he had a five, ten maybe fifteen minute conversation with MG Koster at which time he left and returned to the area of the combat assault. Col. Henderson remained over the area of the operations until about 1030 hours when the C&C helicopter went to Quang Ngai City arriving around 1045 hours for a meeting that Col. Henderson had with Col. Toan.

"I had this interview with Col. Toan which I do not recall how long it lasted, but I do not believe it lasted over twenty minutes. I believe I returned to Duc Pho and had lunch at Duc Pho. That afternoon I was back in the operational area and also visited with my 4/3 Battalion Command Post which was at Fire Support Base Sue which was north of Fire Support Base Dottie."[53]

That afternoon Col. Henderson received a report through his TOC from Task Force Barker that ten to fourteen civilians had been killed. "When I had the report of ten to fourteen from Col. Barker on the afternoon of the 16th it was not my concern that there were a greater number of civilians that may have been killed. I think I had multiplicity of requirements to resweep that village. My thinking that at that time based on what I had observed that morning that I was not satisfied that this body count or whatever it was at that time was accurate or that the number of weapons and that at that time I only assumed that I must have known that there were nine weapons captured since that is what the wall reflects and I had no information from Col. Barker nor did he know as I recall exactly how these civilians had been killed."

When he learned that MG Koster had countermanded his order to resweep My Lai 4, he stated, "I know that I had this feeling that when I first got the report from Col. Barker of ten to twelve civilians having been killed that afternoon that I was greatly concerned about having to report this to my division commander before it even went through my head you are going to be the shortest in time brigade commander in Vietnam because you are being relieved here by nightfall or at least you are going to have a reaming. When I learned that the order had been countermanded the only thing that I wanted to be sure of was that the order that I issued and the purpose of it was understood." [17]

In summary, Col. Henderson arrived at My Lai 4 at 0800 hours, too late to observe the artillery prep or the insertion of Charlie Company. When he flew over the landing zone he saw no bodies. A time budget of his activities that morning included: orbiting two dead VC with weapons; attempting to land to retrieve VC equipment; observing the combat assault of Bravo Company; separating, picking up and flying two detainees to LZ Dottie and returning to My Lai 4; and breaking off to meet MG Koster at LZ Dottie. Between 0800 and 1025 hours when he went to visit Col. Toan, Col. Henderson saw very little of Charlie Companies operation and as a consequence had to rely almost totally upon LTC Barker's portrayal of events.

Observations by Helicopter Occupants

Maj. Robert W. McKnight, 11th Brigade, S-3, related the flight pattern and schedule of events almost identically as told by Col. Henderson. He recalls seeing approximately five bodies, two to the north of the village and three to the south.[54]

LTC Robert B. Luper, the brigade artillery officer when asked if he was aware that some civilians had been killed, responded, "Yes. He could see 15 to 20 bodies along the road leading out of the village some bodies alongside the road. Many of these were women or children.[43]

LTC William I. MacLachlan was the Air Force liaison officer to the 11th Brigade. He recalls the two VC killed north of the village. In the afternoon, he flew over the area in an O-2 aircraft. However, since there were no activities in the My Lai 4 area, he thinks that he would have gone to the area of the 4th/3rd Infantry because the Air Force was getting lots of requests from them at the time. In all, he saw ten or twelve bodies total.[55]

LTC MacLachlan states that it was his function to coordinate air strikes. There were no pre-planned strikes for that day although they had on-calls available. They had no opportunity to place any munitions in the area with Air Force planes.

Specialist Michael C. Adcock was Col. Henderson's radio operator. He saw about six bodies in the village and east of the village along the lips of a ditch Adcock saw about twelve to fifteen bodies, a mixed group of both sexes and all ages. He could identify some as women. One thing that he is absolutely sure of is the bodies in this ditch. In total, Spc. Adcock believes he saw twenty-five to thirty bodies in and around My Lai 4 on 16 March 1968.[56]

Captain James T. Cooney the command pilot for the 11th Brigade recalls they missed all of the insertion of Charlie Company. He remembers seeing only five Vietnamese bodies that day – two north of My Lai 4 immediately upon arrival in the area and three south of My Lai 4 at the junction of the North-South trail and Highway 521. He states that the amount of burning he saw on the day of the operation would be considered a normal amount.[57]

With respect to the body count, all of the other pilots testified they saw a considerable number of Vietnamese bodies in and about My Lai 4 on the 16th of March. Yet those in the command and control saw relatively few. However, when those few that were reported are plotted on an overlay it is apparent that the group in the command and control helicopter saw a maximum of forty-nine. If Henderson in his investigation had questioned the personnel in his own helicopter he would have found from forty-three to forty-nine Vietnamese bodies of which only a few according to the descriptions could have been military. This would have put him on the alert concerning the reports emanating from Task Force Barker.

With respect to the burning of houses, Col. Henderson observed three or four houses burning, and questioned LTC Barker about it. When he arrived on station at 0930 hours Culverhouse noticed that the village was on fire. Lt. Alaux states "… at the time we went through the village most of the hooches were on fire …" Considering the photographs taken by Mr. Haeberle, there are major differences in observations. Testimony has indicated that the torching of the Vietnamese hamlets by the 11th Brigade soldiers had occurred previously, leading one to consider that the troops were not "exceptionally well trained" nor as disciplined as their former brigade commander believed.

<u>Radio Traffic</u>
Capt. Charles R. Lewellen[58] was the Assistant S-3 of Task Force Barker. He was the TOC night duty officer on 15 March 1968 and was relieved sometime between 0630 and 0700 hours by Maj. Calhoun. Capt. Lewellen taped the operation on a Japanese made, battery operated, Toshiba tape recorder. He went into the TOC where the radios were on a corner table, and put his tape recorder on a bench and held the microphone near the radios. He was in the TOC from the time the operation started until about 0930 hours at which time MG Koster arrived in the TOC and Capt. Lewellen quit taping and left. Perusal of the conversations on this tape which were mostly the transmissions on the air-ground frequency might lead one to believe that there was nothing unusual concerning the operation. Yet, there were no requests for helicopter, artillery or tactical air support nor were there any references to enemy bunkers or positions that need softening up or any indication of enemy fire being received. It sounded more like a stroll in the park.

Mr. James H. Flynn[24] was forward observer for the 4.2 mortar, C/1-20. According to Mr. Flynn, Capt. Medina called all of the platoon leaders and told them to stop the killing. Before lunch Mr. Flynn heard Capt. Medina making a transmission referencing body count. He said there was 300; or something like that."

Mr. Lawrence J. Kubert[61] remembers an earlier transmission from the light observation helicopter that was in the area. These were "There are a lot of bodies down there". Maj. Watke asked "How many bodies" and the reply was "About 150 to 200 bodies". They also said, "I came over the ditch and all I saw were bodies". When asked about weapons, the reply was there were no weapons, but that there were women, children, and old men. Mr. Kubert stated the call sign making this report was "Skeeter" and would have been WO Thompson.

Private Kinch,[22] an 81mm mortarman assigned to Company C, was on the ground during the 16 March operation at My Lai 4. Pvt. Kinch stated that Capt. Medina received a call from someone saying that the medevac said there were bodies all over the place. The person wanted to know why. Capt. Medina said that he did not know, but he would find out. Pvt. Kinch also remembers as they were walking along the path there was a body count called for and Capt. Medina said 310. Pvt. Kinch said he could remember it because he was shocked by the figure at the time.

SSG Martin Fagan[40] the chief fire direction computer of the 81mm mortar platoon was on the ground with Company C on 16 March and remembers a specific radio transmission by Capt. Medina asking higher headquarters for a change from a search and destroy mission. According to SSG Fagan Capt. Medina said something like "There don't seem to be many NVA or VC in the village. I want to change the mission from search and destroy to search and clear."

Capt. Kotouc[19], the Task Force Barker S-2, remembers a transmission about a boy running across the road and someone shooting him with a machine gun. He cannot recall Maj. Calhoun's exact reply, but it was to tell them to be careful and to be sure who they shot. Either the company commander or C-81, the relay on LZ Uptight, "Rogered" Maj. Calhoun's reply.

CSM Roy D. Kirkpatrick[63] the chief operations sergeant of the 11th Brigade recalls an unusual radio call being monitored in the TOC. He heard a portion on one of the radios in the S-3 Air Section and the portion of the radio transmission he heard was "If you shoot him, I'll shoot you". His thoughts were what was going on there. The duty officer made a call by land line to Task Force Barker to see what was going on.

CSM James D. Rogers,[64] the American Division sergeant major, was flying with MG Koster that day and remembers the order to go back in and get a body count. They were to distinguish the enemy, how they were killed, and how many females. MG Koster countermanded this order. He does not know of another case where MG Koster countermanded an order. Also he could not ever remember hearing another request for a body count to include women.

Spc. Kubert, the acting Operations Sergeant at LZ Dottie for the 123rd Aviation Company, monitored the radios and administered records. He kept a historical journal for the company as an official duty. He is sure he put the 16 March operation in the report because he couldn't figure out what to say. He believes he wrote the following: The Aero Scouts discovered 150 bodies of women and children in this area without weapons. There is no indication as to how they were killed. Unfortunately all the 123rd documents for the 16-19 March 1968 period are missing.[61]

In an over-flight of the areas of operations MG Koster was obviously monitoring the Task Force Barker command net. It is not known which of those unusual transmissions he overheard but something compelled him to ask "What is going on down there?"

To anyone monitoring radio nets, and Col. Henderson testified he tried to monitor the active nets, the totality of the aforementioned traffic, which is not all inclusive, should have raised the gravest suspicions concerning Task Force Barker Operation. There was a lot of chatter about shooting and killing but none about essential maneuver and firepower! The assault was not contested and the reported numbers of combatants killed were contrived data from Capt. Medina and LTC Barker.

Summary of Charlie Companies Assault
Charlie Company, new to South Vietnam, spent the month previous to the My Lai assault patrolling the countryside searching for an enemy they could not distinguish from local villagers. They began to take serious casualties from an enemy they could not see and became frustrated and angry. The evening prior to the assault Capt. Medina called his company together to brief and to motivate them. The company was told they were to burn the houses, kill the livestock and level the hamlet. Many erroneously interpreted those instructions to include the killing of everyone. Medina's efforts to psych-up his inexperienced troops exceeded his expectations. So the next morning the psyched-up, frustrated, angry, scared and highly motivated group started out on their first combat assault. Upon entering My Lai they started to randomly kill the inhabitants, burn the houses and even to rape some women. That morning Charlie Company slaughtered over 400 civilians and leveled the hamlet.

Supporting division aviators promptly reported through the chain of command that about 100 non-combatant casualties had been observed. Whereas, LTC Barker and Capt. Medina both forcibly reported Charlie Company was engaged in a contested battle with an enemy located in bunkered positions where 128 VC were killed and 20 non-combatant casualties resulted from artillery and gunship fires.

That day there were no requests for artillery, gunship or air force support nor was there any tactical radio chatter that one would expect in a contested fight against a bunkered enemy that experienced heavy casualties. In fact, there was no enemy, only unarmed elderly men, women and children.

It is interesting to see how the situation on 16 March was duly reported by participants and observers.

REPORTING THE OPERATION

It is obvious from the foregoing that the soldiers of Charlie Company had violated the Laws of War by the wanton killing of unarmed civilians and the indiscriminate destruction of property. General Westmoreland noted that none of these atrocious acts had previously surfaced in Vietnam and being very concerned he directed the investigation whose purpose was: to determine if the incidents at My Lai 4 were reported; if reported, were they properly investigated; and if investigated, was there a cover-up. This section will discuss the reporting, or lack of reporting, of these incidents to higher authority.

1. <u>WO Thompson</u> to <u>Maj Watke</u> to <u>Holladay</u> to <u>BG Young</u> to <u>MG Koster</u>
    (pilot)   (Co CO)   (Bn CO)   (ADC)   (CG)

Warrant Officer Thompson returned to LZ Dottie from the hospital at Quang Ngai about noon on 16 March. After shutting down the aircraft he went to the operations van to see Maj. Frederick W. Watke, who was the Commanding Officer, Company B, 123rd Aviation Battalion. WO Thompson told him about the captain shooting the woman, the bunker, the ditch, the sergeant pointing his weapon into the ditch full of people and evacuating a child to the hospital. The child in the ditch upset him the most and he is certain he told Maj. Watke about that. Maj. Watke was very concerned that his people had entered into a heated argument, so to speak, with the ground troops, and this was an untenable situation. Maj. Watke said that Mr. Thompson was coherent, normal and was not emotionally disturbed when he made his report but he was basically very firm in what he was saying and this thing really bothered him. Watke never again questioned Mr. Thompson, Mr. Millians or the others concerning what had happened at My Lai 4.

Maj. Watke related that fifteen to thirty minutes after his talk with Mr. Thompson he informed LTC Barker concerning the incident, telling him in effect what Mr. Thompson had said. LTC Barker seemed to be quite concerned about the entire matter and he called for his helicopter to go out into the area to look into the situation – obviously to talk to Capt. Medina.

In the evening Maj. Watke reported to his battalion commander, LTC

Holladay, at division headquarters in Chu Lai. It was about 2000 hours when he told him what had transpired. LTC Holladay repeatedly asked Maj. Watke if he realized the magnitude of this story and he stated that he did. LTC Holladay had confidence that Watke would give him only a complete version of the story. The two of them agonized what should be done and Holladay said he would have to go to BG Young his immediate superior. Since it was then about midnight, because of the late hour he waited until the next morning, 17 March.

LTC Holladay[65] and Major Watke went to see BG Young about 0730 hours the following morning. LTC Holladay informed BG Young that he had some information the general should know and asked Maj. Watke to relate the same story that he had told the night before. BG Young was profoundly concerned about the story. He seemed much more concerned about the confrontation between WO Thompson and LT Calley than the large number of civilians being killed. BG Young did not give any directions as to what they should do but he gave the impression that he would take care of it.

In the normal course of events, the Chief of Staff was informed. LTC Holladay told Col. Parson about the incident after the evening briefing at 1700 hours on 17 March. Parson was shocked and he said, "My God, that's murder! Here we are trying to help these people and we are doing this sort of thing."

Later on 17 March, LTC Holladay and Maj. Watke had a meeting at Duc Pho shortly after noon with Col. Henderson to resolve differences in the philosophy of the use of the aero scout company. The incident of 16 March surprisingly was not mentioned to Col. Henderson at that meeting. Holladay did not want to mention it to Col. Henderson because of the enormity of it, it would have been unpleasant and disagreeable to discuss. It might have been common courtesy to inform Col. Henderson of this incident before BG Young discussed it with him. LTC Holladay had no reason to believe that Col. Henderson did or did not know about the incident at that time and actually he was relieved when Col. Henderson did not bring the subject up.

Brigadier General George H. Young assumed duty as Assistant Division Commander for Maneuver of the Americal Division on 15 March 1968. Previously from November 1967 he had been Assistant Division Commander for Support. The first BG Young heard of Task Force Barker operation at My Lai 4 was during the evening briefing at division headquarters on 16 March. Maj. Watke's reporting the morning of 17

March concerned BG Young for two reasons: first, if the ground forces were carrying out their orders concerning the safekeeping of non-combatants and second that American troops might be firing on other American troops. BG Young stated that he did not recall hearing about fifty to one hundred bodies in a ditch, a dark complexioned captain killing a woman, a colored sergeant standing over the ditch, or any non-combatant civilians being brought out of the area by helicopter. BG Young reported the incident to MG Koster about noon on the 17th of March who instructed him to direct Col. Henderson to make an investigation. Koster could just as well have directed his staff to investigate. There was a sense of urgency with regard to this matter.[66]

Major General Samuel W. Koster was Division Commander of the Americal Division from September 1967 to June 1968. He states that the story of the helicopter pilot was brought to him about noon on what was reconstructed for him as the 17th of March 1968. BG Young was the one who told MG Koster the story and Koster always had the feeling that there was somebody else there and the most likely person was Col. Parson. Young related that he had heard the story from Maj. Watke and LTC Holladay.

It is important to note that a time honored principle in the United States Army concerning the use of the chain of command worked with respect to the incidents alleged to have occurred at My Lai 4 on 16 March by Warrant Officer Thompson. By noon the next day the commanding general of the Americal Division personally heard about the Warrant Officer's allegation. The report that General Koster received included: indiscriminate firing; confrontation by Warrant Officer and ground troop leader; evacuation of civilians that Warrant Officer felt were in danger; that he had seen some bodies; and somebody had been evacuated to Quang Ngai hospital. Three of the elements in WO Thompson's allegations were not recalled by MG Koster almost one and one-half years later: the shooting of the woman by a captain, the large number of bodies in the ditch and a sergeant pointing his weapon in the ditch. In all probability these three incidents were not briefed to the commanding general. Based on the information that he received through the chain of command MG Koster directed an investigation be made.

2.   Col. Henderson   to   MG Koster
         (Bde CO)   (CG)

When Col. Henderson met MG Koster at LZ Dottie at about 0935 hours on the 16th, he discussed the VC detainees that he had picked up and mentioned the group of civilians who were evacuating the area. "MG Koster asked 'Have you got any reports of any civilians being injured?' and Henderson informed him 'No, I don't have any reports from Col. Barker of any civilians being injured up to this point. However, I personally observed six to eight bodies in the area, some of which might be civilians.' And his instructions to me were, 'Well I hope no other --- let's don't get anybody hurt. Ask Barker to give you a report and relay it to me'." Col. Henderson believes he had maybe a fifteen minute conversation with MG Koster at which time he left and returned to the area of the combat assault.[17]

3.   <u>Capt. Medina</u>   to   <u>MG Koster</u>
         (Co CO)   (CG)

At about 1600 hours on the afternoon of the 16th Task Force Barker received a call from brigade directing them to resweep My Lai 4 to count the number of non-combatant casualties. According to Capt. Medina, "Maj. Calhoun told me to go back to My Lai 4, and he wanted to know how many women and children, innocent civilians, had been killed, if any, and he wanted me to go back to My Lai 4 and make a body count, women, children, and men. I stated that I did not think that it would be wise for me to start moving from the defensive position to My Lai 4 to do this because of the distance involved. About that time the commanding general was in the vicinity somewhere with his helicopter -- ... Sabre 6, I believe, was his call sign ... I know he was in the area because he broke in on the – he came in on the radio and he said, 'Negative. I do not. Don't send them back there. I don't want them going through that mess.' He says, 'What does the captain say the number of civilians that he saw killed was?' and I gave him a count of twenty to twenty-eight and he said, 'Well that sounds about right,' and that was it."[23]

4.   <u>LTC Barker</u>   to <u>Col. Henderson</u>   to   <u>MG Koster</u>
         (Bn CO)   (Bde CO)   (CG)

On the evening of 16 March Col. Henderson recalls getting a report of the number of non-combatant civilian casualties resulting from the operation from LTC Barker. Immediately following he called MG Koster and related that he had information that there were twenty non-combatant casualties resulting from the operation.

These aforementioned reports given to MG Koster all dealt with the same subject, non-combatant casualties, and all originated from different personnel in the chain of command.

5. <u>WO Thompson</u> to <u>Capt. Creswell</u> to <u>LTC Lewis</u> to <u>Col Parson</u>
    (pilot)   (Chap)   (Div Chap)   (CofS)

Capt. Creswell was the division artillery chaplain of the American Division. He knew WO Thompson very well since he had flown him many times in the performance of Creswell's duties. Chaplain Creswell relates, "To the best of my recollection on March 17th, 1968, WO Hugh Thompson came to see me, which Thompson was very upset ... Thompson told me that he flew a slick (chopper without guns) for a combat assault on a small village called My Lai 4. Upon a later return to the My Lai 4 area he had seen a large number of bodies, in excess of 160. Upon making passes over the area, it seemed to Thompson that most of the bodies were women and children."

WO Thompson indicated that he was going to report what had happened through command channels. Chaplain Creswell recalls, Thompson went through his command channels and he went through chaplain channels. On the basis of Thompson's allegations and his own observations at Task Force Barker Headquarters, he went to the division chaplain, LTC Frances Lewis. It is Creswell's opinion that the investigation was superficial at best and there never was an attempt at division level to prove or disprove Mr. Thompson's allegations regarding the My Lai 4 operation.[20]

LTC Francis Lewis, the American Division chaplain,[67] recalled the My Lai 4 incident because Capt. Creswell, one of his chaplains, visited his office on 17 March 1968 to report a conversation with a warrant officer who had flown in the My Lai 4 Operation. The warrant officer reported that there was unnecessary killing of civilians at My Lai 4. No numbers were listed.

LTC Lewis[67] kept a journal of his activities and he remembers his journal stating he saw both LTC Balmer, the G-3, and LTC Trexler, the G-2, and told them what Capt. Creswell had told him. LTC Balmer said he had heard something about this operation and it would be looked into. LTC Lewis mentioned to LTC Balmer and LTC Trexler that there were unnecessary shootings and he also mentioned about a soldier shooting the civilians. LTC Lewis feels that both understood what he was talking about immediately and he believes that it was not discussed in detail because it was their business to know it. He does not feel that he got a brush-off.

LTC Lewis discussed the incident several times with the Chief of Staff, Colonel Parson. Col. Parson on these occasions gave him indications that the matter was being investigated. Not long afterwards, LTC Lewis informed LTC Anistranski, the G-5, who normally got into the act wherever non-combatants were involved. Yet Anistranski never briefed about this incident as he did other incidents.

Besides the chain of command reporting to division headquarters the technical chain working through the chaplains also operated expeditiously. The division commander as well as his principal staff officer, the chief of staff, and some key subordinates of the chief of staff had word of the allegations of WO Thompson by the 17th of March.

6. LTC Barker to   MG Koster
       (Bn CO)   (CG)

On the 18th MG Koster[68] visited LZ Dottie from 1345 to 1420 hours because he wanted to talk to Col. Barker firsthand to find out what his story was. After all, LTC Barker was commander of the Task Force and was in charge of the operation and knew best what they had done on the ground. MG Koster stated that Barker assured him that the troops had conducted themselves properly. Additionally, MG Koster had visited Task Force Barker at LZ Dottie twice on 16 March.

7. Task Force Barker Log to   11th Brigade Log to Division Log

Several pertinent extracts from the three operational journals of the units involved in the 16 March My Lai 4 operation (Task Force Barker, 11th Brigade and the American Division) are shown subsequently. The key entries for comparison of the journal items are those of Task Force Barker and in each case the Task Force Barker entry is traced through the 11th Brigade log to the American Division log.

Item	Time	TF Barker	Item	Time	11th Brigade	Item	Time	American Division
16	0758	Co C killed 14 VC vic 716788, had documents and ammo pouches (notified 11th Bde)	39	0805	TFB/TOC; C/1-20, 0757, 716788; engaged unk number of VC, results 14 VC KIA. Loc doc, 2 carbines CIA, 1 M-1 rifle CIA, 1 H/G CIA and assorted web hear CIA. Will evac (notified S-2, S-3, DTOC 0810)	10	0808	11th, C/1-20 vic BS 716788 at 0750 hrs located documents and equip, 14 VC KIA (G-3, C/S, III MAF, M notified)

| 22 | 0840 | Co C has counted 69 VC killed vic 716788 (11th Bde notified) | 53 | 0935 | TFB/TOC, 0930 hrs C/1-20 714794 counted 69 VC KIA as a result of arty fire (notified S-2, S-3, DTOC at 0940 | 28 | 0940 | (Delayed) 11, C/1-20 vic BS714794 at 0930 hrs elements counted 69 VC KIA as a result of arty fire this morning. In process of policing up wpns and equip additional bodies from previous counts (G-3, C/S, G-2, III MAF notified) |
| 39 | 1555 | Co B reports that none of the VC body count reported by his unit were women and children, Co C reports that approx 10 to 11 women and children were killed either by arty or gun ships. These were not included in body count (11th Bde notified) | | | No Entry | | | No entry |

Perusal of the logs indicates that rarely was there a time sequence problem. For example, Item 16 of the Task Force Barker journal indicates "Charlie Company killed 14 VC" and it is entered at 0758. It is also noted at 0805 in the 11th Brigade log and at 0808 in the American Division journal. However, when one's attention is called to Item 22 of the Task Force Barker journal where "Co C has counted sixty-nine VC killed vic 716788", it is unusual to find that this major piece of what might be considered highly reportable good news was not transmitted to the 11th Brigade until sometime between 0930 and 0935 hours, some fifty minutes later. Of more importance is the fact that when it was finally transmitted that the coordinates had been changed from 716788 which is the center of My Lai 4 to 714794 which is an open field hundreds of meters further to the northwest. There was more to this entry than meets the eye. The actual report that came over the radio was monitored by Capt. Lewellen's tape when shortly after 0827 hours Coyote 6 (LTC Barker), in conversation

believed to be with Charlie Company on the ground, was heard to say
"Coyote Six. Is that eight .. ah eight four KIA's. Over." SFC Stephens,
the S-2 sergeant of Task Force Barker recalls that LTC Barker came into
the TOC and Maj. Calhoun explained that they had counted fifteen VC
killed up until that time, so they subtracted these from the eighty-four body
count and there were sixty-nine left.[16] None of the fifteen VC previously
reported had been killed by artillery and a decision was made to credit the
sixty-nine body count to artillery. It can be noted that Item 22 in Task
Force Barker log makes no reference to artillery fire. It can only be
presumed that between 0840 when this item was entered and 0930 hours
when it was called to the 11th Brigade that a decision had been made not
only to credit the body count to artillery but to change the coordinates from
716788 to 714794. Although there were five errors of transposition of
coordinates in the log that day, this change appeared to be more than a
clerical error because the division newspaper account of the fight stated
they counted sixty-nine enemy bodies in marshes a mile west of My Lai 4.
The official version had been changed from My Lai 4 to the marshes.
None of the artillery personnel involved reported any body count and it is
highly doubtful that a five minute artillery preparation using point
detonating fuse could have killed sixty-nine enemy in entrenched positions.
The report of sixty-nine VC killed by artillery was a continued attempt by
LTC Barker to draw attention away from the indiscriminant killing of
Vietnamese by small arms fire. Thus the cover-up began one hour after the
troops landed.

Another item of interest is Item 39 of Task Force Barker journal where it
relates "… Company C reports that approx. ten to eleven women and
children were killed by either artillery or gunships. These were not included
in body count." According to Task Force Barker log, the 11th Brigade was
notified, yet there is no entry in the 11th Brigade or American Division
journals. Col. Henderson before this investigation stated that he received a
report through his TOC from Task Force Barker that ten to fourteen
civilians had been killed. The fact that non-combatant casualties were not
reported in the brigade and division logs precluded a follow-on report of
non-combatant casualties by the division to MACV which would have
raised a red flag on the operation.

8. Task Force Barker Combat Action Report to Division Headquarters[69]

On 19 March the American Division Headquarters requested a Combat
Action Report from the 11th Infantry Brigade concerning the operation of
the 1st Battalion 20th Infantry in the vicinity BX7179 on 16 March 1968.
LTC Barker prepared a full scale Combat Action Report dated 28 March

1968 which, according to Maj. Calhoun he wrote himself. Two portions of Barker's report are reproduced:

"Entry 11. Execution: The order was issued on 14 March 1968. Coordination with supporting arms reconnaissance and positioning of forces was conducted on 15 March 1968. On 160726 March 1968 a three minute artillery preparation began on the first landing zone and 0730 hours the first lift for Co C touched down while helicopter gunships provided suppressive fires. At 0747 hours the last lift of Co C was completed. The initial preparation resulted in sixty-eight VC KIA's in the enemy's combat outpost positions. Co C then immediately attacked to the east receiving enemy small arms fire as they pressed forward" and
"Entry 15. Commander Analysis: This operation was well planned, well executed and successful. Friendly casualties were light and the enemy suffered heavily. On this operation the civilian population supporting the VC in the area numbered approximately 200. This created a problem in population control and medical care of those civilians caught in fires of the opposing forces. However, the infantry unit on the ground and helicopters were able to assist civilians in leaving the area and in caring for and/or evacuating the wounded."

The first item of interest with respect to this report is the fact that division headquarters singled out only Charlie Company of the three company units involved in the 16 March operation to make a report. This may indicate some knowledge at division headquarters concerning the operation on 16 March. The Combat Action Report was prepared by LTC Barker personally and had two large omissions. First, it did not mention non-combatant casualties. Second, there was no mention of the burning of houses. LTC Barker's later analysis that, "This operation was well planned, well executed and successful", indicates a desire on his part to gloss over the operation in official channels.

LTC Barker's report instead of referring to the Charlie Company operation on 16 March as requested where there were no enemy inflicted casualties, covered all units in the four day operation and listed 2 US killed and 11 US wounded, of which all but one self-inflicted wound occurred in Bravo Company. Barker also reported Charlie Company was "receiving small arms fire." The report was blatantly false. It left the desired impression of a contested battle and is undoubtedly a major reason why the higher echelon personnel did not dig deeper into the Charlie Company activities.

9. <u>Public Information Representatives</u> to <u>Division Newspaper</u>

As indicated previously two members of the 31st PIO Detachment, Specialists Haeberle and Roberts, accompanied Task Force Barker on their 16 March operation. They submitted their report in time to make the front page story on The Americal News Sheet for Sunday, 17 March. Two portions of this news article are reproduced. "Chu Lai (Americal IO) – A combat assault into a hot LZ started the day off right for infantrymen in the Task Force Barker area of Operation Muscatine yesterday. By mid-afternoon when the enemy broke contact Americal's 11th Brigade soldiers with support from artillery and gunships had killed 128 Viet Cong. The 128 enemy dead was the largest enemy body count recorded by the 11th Brigade for a twenty-four hour period since they took control of Operation Muscatine. It also is the largest number killed by the "Jungle Warriors" in one day's fighting since they became a part of the Americal Division. ... As the "Warriors" moved through the marshes several hundred meters west of My Lai they counted sixty-nine enemy bodies killed by a battery of the 6th Battalion, 11th Artillery. The battery commanded by Capt. Steven Gamble (Portsmouth, N.H.), fired on the enemy from a location approximately three miles to the north."

Haeberle and Roberts both returned to LZ Dottie in the afternoon of 16 March and visited the TOC. Roberts testified that LTC Barker came along, invited him in and gave him an interview. He explained, using maps, the military concept of the operations. It is obvious that Roberts' report of sixty-nine VC killed by artillery in the marshes one mile west of My Lai 4 came from LTC Barker who desperately needed a falsified newspaper article to support his cover-up endeavours.[70]

When the story in the Americal News Sheet is compared against Specialist Haeberle's and Specialist Roberts' statements it is noted that there is little correlation between what they reported and what they actually saw in the field. Why they elected to participate in the cover-up is difficult to comprehend.

10. <u>Letter Report, Census Grievance</u> to <u>Census Grievance Committee</u>
       <u>Committee Cadreman</u>   <u>Chief Province Headquarters</u>[71]

On 18 March a Census Grievance Committee Cadreman submitted a report through Rural Development channels to his boss at Quang Ngai Province that 427 civilians and guerrillas were killed in a three day operation at Tu Cung (My Lai 4) hamlet, including young and old. At the time this report was made the allied operations were still going on in the vicinity. The

significance of this is that a thorough contact with Vietnamese officials during the course of an investigation should have been able to ascertain this data.

11. Report from Son Tinh District Chief to Province Chief, Quang Ngai[72]

The District Chief of Son Tinh heard reports concerning what had transpired on 16 March at My Lai 4 (Son My Village) and submitted a report in letter form whose subject was Confirmation of Allied Troops Shooting at the Residents of Tu Cung Hamlet, Coordinates BS 721795. The observation of the District Chief is quoted subsequently, "Observation by this headquarters: The Tu Cung Hamlet and the neighboring hamlets, e.g., My Lai (BS 737800) and Van Thien (BS 794804), in Son My Village had become insecure since 1964, so the administrative authorities of these area had been forced to flee to Son Long (BS 638754), leaving these hamlets under VC control. Casualties were unavoidably caused to the hamlet's residents during the firefight, while the local administrative authorities were not present in the area. The enemy may take advantage of this incident to undermine, through fallacious propaganda, the prestige of the RVNAF, and frustrate the government's rural pacification efforts. Respectfully yours". Copies of this report from 1st Lt. Tran Ngoc Tan were sent to the S-2 and S-3, Quang Ngai Sector Headquarters.

12. Report from Son Tinh District Chief to Province Chief, Quang Ngai[73]

Again, on 11 April, the District Chief of Son Tinh District submitted another letter report to the Province Chief whose subject was, Allied Operation at Son My assembled and killed civilians. Again, the observation of the subsector is quoted, "Subsector comments. Tu Cung and Co Loy are two areas of Son My Village that have long been held by the VC. The district forces lack the capability of entering the area. Therefore, allied units frequently conduct mop-up operations and bombing attacks freely in the area. But the basic position of the report of the Son My Village committee is that although the VC cannot be held blameless for their actions in the 16 March 1968 operation, the Americans in anger killed too many civilians. Only one American was killed by the VC, however the allied killed near 500 civilians in retaliation. Really an atrocious attitude if it cannot be called an act of insane violence. Request you intervene on behalf of the people." Copies of this second report from 1st Lt. Tran Ngoc Tan were sent to 2nd ARVN division headquarters, MACV Quang Ngai sector, and the Major US Advisor, Son Tinh Subsection.

When the 28 March and the 11 April reports of Lt. Tran Ngoc Tan, the Son Tinh District Chief, are compared it is seen that there was a great change of attitude at the Vietnamese district level concerning what transpired at My Lai 4 – that is, "an act of insane violence."

13. <u>Letter Report from Assistant</u>   to   <u>Senior Advisor Quang Ngai</u>
      <u>District Son Tinh Advisor</u>   <u>Province to American Division</u>[74]

Captain Angel M. Rodriguez was the assistant district advisor of the Son Tinh District. He had received information from province that they wanted the substance of Lt. Tan's 11 April letter investigated. Therefore, Capt. Rodriguez discussed this letter with Lt. Tan.[75] "I received the letter from the headquarters, I took the copy and I studied it and then I waited until I had the opportunity to talk to then Lt. Tan, because he was the originator of that letter. I discussed it with him and I prepared a draft, I sat down and typed the statement that you have mentioned before and I sent it to the headquarters." When asked if he believed the accusations or allegations in Lt. Tan's letter, Capt. Rodriguez said he did not. "Because when I read this accusation, it never came into my mind that the American troops, especially the Americal Division, I had admiration for those people, they wouldn't do something like that." Capt. Rodriguez forwarded his letter to province. The gist of Capt. Rodriguez' statement is quoted as follows: "The Son Tinh District Chief received a letter from the Village Chief of Son My Village containing the complaint of the killing of 490 civilians including children and women by American troops. The Village Chief alleged that an American unit operating in the area on 16 March 1968 and killed these civilians with their own personal weapons."

Specialist John W. Hill, Secretary to the Chief of Staff, Americal Division[76], remembers that "Captain Rodriguez, brought a report concerning the complaint that had been made by a Vietnamese civilian into the Command headquarters and gave it to Colonel Parson."

Captain Rodriguez' report is the first available official US document in advisory channels that relates to the incident at My Lai 4. This report was prepared on 14 April and uses as its base the Son Tinh District Chief's letter citing the killing of over 500 civilians including children and women by American troops. Capt. Rodriguez' letter was hand-delivered to the Americal Division Headquarters sometime in mid-April and was also attached to Colonel Henderson's 24 April report.

14. <u>VC Propaganda Message</u>   to   <u>Americal Division</u>

The VC took advantage of the incident at My Lai to undermine the efforts of the Vietnamese and US governments. In a propaganda message entitled "The Americans Devils Devulge True Form", in one paragraph stated "In the operation of 15 March 1968 in Son Tinh District the American enemies went crazy. They used machine guns and every other kind of weapons to kill 500 people who had empty hands, in Tin Kho (Son My) Village (Son Tinh District, Quang Ngai Province). There were many pregnant women some of which were only a few days from childbirth. The Americans would shoot everybody they saw. They killed people and cows, burned homes. There were some families in which all members were killed."[77]

LTC Blackledge, the 11th Brigade Intelligence Officer, recalls seeing two VC propaganda documents. The first document was similar in content to one attached to the 24 April report and it was obtained about mid-April. When he obtained these documents, he showed them to Col. Henderson. The documents were distributed to division headquarters as well as to brigade. LTC Blackledge stated that this VC propaganda report was unusual because it referred to a unit by name, the date, time and place. It was not the general type of report, rather it was specific.

The responses of the Vietnamese Provencial Authorties to the various reports of the 16 March operation are of interest. All the Vietnamese governmental organizations in Quang Ngai Province were expeditiously informed of the destruction and killings at My Lai 4. As early as 18 March while the operation was ongoing a Rural Development census grievance cadreman reported to his chief at Quang Ngai that 427 civilians including women and children were killed at Son My Village. Shortly thereafter on 22 March the Son My Village chief reported to Son Tinh District chief that 570 civilians were killed and animals, property and houses were 90 percent destroyed. The Son Tinh District chief, 1st Lt. Tran Ngoc Tan, on 28 March in a letter to the Quang Ngai Province chief reported this was fallacious VC propaganda. However, on 11 April in another letter to the province chief with a copy to the 2nd ARVN Division Lt. Tan changed his opinion and wrote the My Lai 4 operation was "really an atrocious attitude if it can not be called an act of insane violence". About mid April the VC distributed a leaflet titled "The American Devils Divulge Their True Form" wherein it said "… the American enemies went crazy… to kill 500 people who had empty hands."

The VC propaganda leaflet and the report of the Son Tinh District chief were forwarded in Vietnamese channels to Col. Nguyen Van Toan, the CG

2nd ARVN Division, by his G-2 on 12 April. Col. Toan most probably was not greatly concerned that the VC stronghold of My Lai 4 was virtually destroyed since it was the general location of the 48th VC Local Force Battalion headquarters which since 1964 had been a proverbial thorn in the government's side. Because this matter was of primary interest to the Quang Ngai province chief he sent a letter to LTC Khien on 15 April requesting him to review the incident. LTC Khien was of the opinion that the VC leaflet and the local reports were propaganda and was lukewarm towards ordering a vigorous investigation. Both MG Koster and Col. Henderson subsequent to their receipts of the VC propaganda leaflet separately visited both Col. Toan and LTC Khien where they were advised that there was probably no substance to the VC claims. This was an important factor in allaying their fears that something untoward had occurred at My Lai 4. Consider that Col. Toan's and LTC Khien's assumptions could be considered rational, for who could believe that American troops would purposely machine gun and wantonly kill over 400 innocent civilians, predominantly women and children. The Viet Cong cried wolf about almost every incident. However, with respect to My Lai 4, their propaganda was correct, yet the Vietnamese provincial authorities didn't believe it. The incident was never investigated by the Vietnamese authorities and was soon forgotten.

Summary of the Reporting
Eighteen separate reporting actions reached the Americal Division headquarters. This includes the fourteen listed plus LTC Holladay's report to Chief of Staff and LTC Lewis' reports to G-2, G-3 and G-5. Thirteen of these eighteen reports were completed prior to 20 March and five were completed subsequently. Thirteen of these went through US channels, one was through USMACV advisory channels, three were through Vietnamese channels to the Quang Ngai Province Chief and one was a VC Propaganda message. All the organizations supporting the Vietnamese Pacification Program were involved in the reporting of the My Lai 4 operation – Americal Division, 2nd ARVN Division, Quang Ngai Province, Son Tinh District, Rural Development Cadre, and CORDS advisors.

The reports obtained through Vietnamese official channels, and the VC propaganda leaflet all contained details of hundreds of civilians killed. With the exception of the letter report from the Census Grievance Committee Cadreman, these were written after 20 March. The disdain which the senior Vietnamese government officials in Quang Ngai Province had for the rural communists was manifested by their feeble attempts to look into the reports of the census grievance cadremen, the Son Tinh District and the VC propaganda. It is difficult to understand why the US province advisors and the 2nd ARVN Division did not forward the content of the Vietnamese reports to their higher headquarters, particularly when both MG Koster and Col. Henderson thought the reports were of such interest that they independently visited both Col. Toan and LTC Thien to discuss them. Had they been forwarded it is possible that a more thorough investigation would have been ordered.

The first report on non-combatant casualties in Americal Division channels was made by Col. Henderson to MG Koster about 0930 hours of the morning of Charlie Company's combat assault. Subsequently, prior to noon on the 16th WO Thompson, a helicopter pilot, reported to his commanding officer Maj. Watke, that he observed over 100 non-combatant bodies lying on the ground during the task force operation. By the next morning MG Koster had been informed of Thompson's observation.

The reporting of the non-combatant casualties at My Lai 4 was good. The chain of command, brigade, battalion and company reported that non-combatants had been killed on the 16th, although LTC Barker and Capt. Medina purposely failed to describe the reality of the situation. Nevertheless, the command section and the general staff at Americal Division headquarters all were aware by 17 March that numerous non-combatants had been killed but not the extent of the killing.

There was a serious difference in the reports received. The Vietnamese and WO Thompson reported hundreds of civilian casualties resulting from indiscriminate troop firings, whereas LTC Barker and Capt. Medina were reporting a 128 VC body count and 20 civilians killed by artillery and gunships. This dichotomy had to be sorted out and it is important to review the actions taken by the division headquarters upon receipt of the information to resolve this issue.

ACTIONS TAKEN BY THE AMERICAL DIVISION HEADQUARTERS

MACV regulations required military personnel to report serious incidents such as the killing of civilians to their commanding officer as soon as possible, that is, to utilize the chain of command. By March 17th, only one day after the initial combat assault and while the Task Force Barker operation was still ongoing, the commanding general, his deputy and the general staff of the Americal Division had all been informed of the killings of Vietnamese non-combatants. The chain of command had operated expeditiously. Now it was the duty of the Americal Division headquarters to further report this incident to MACV headquarters and if it believed the situation was serious enough to initiate an investigation. The actions taken by the division headquarters are discussed subsequently.

For this review it is helpful to discuss the headquarters organization. The management of an infantry division comprised of 15,000 troops and their complex equipment that is engaged in a guerrilla war in the countryside of Vietnam is a challenging task. The division headquarters was instrumental in assisting MG Koster in this endeavor. Basically the headquarters consisted of three elements: the command section; the general staff; the special staff, all supported by administrative elements. The command section included the division commander and two brigadier deputies. BG Young was the Assistant Division Commander for maneuver. Those members of the general staff associated with the combat assault were: the G-2 (intelligence); the G-3 (operations); the G-5 (civil affairs); and the aviation officer who also commanded the aviation battalion. The special staff members normally involved in affairs of good order and discipline were: the staff judge advocate; the provost marshal; the inspector general; and the chaplain. The chief of staff supported the command section and supervised the general and special staffs.

The Command Section

MG Samuel W. Koster, the Americal Division Commander, flew in his command and control helicopter over the area of operations in the vicinity of My Lai shortly after 0900 on 16 March 1968. As was his custom while he was over the area he monitored the command net or some net within the area of operations. At approximately this time the gunship platoon leader heard Sabre 6 (MG Koster's radio identification) ask the question, "What's going on down there?" MG Koster then flew into LZ Dottie arriving at 0935. He was met at the chopper pad by Col. Henderson and they discussed the operation. One of the things they discussed was the two POW's that Col. Henderson had just picked up on the ground and brought back for interrogation. MG Koster either saw or perhaps Col. Henderson related to him that there were many civilians moving. He was sure that he would have seen this. Col. Henderson related to MG Koster that he personally had seen non-combatant casualties numbering approximately six to eight and they had a discussion concerning the safekeeping of non-combatant casualties. Evidence seems to indicate that MG Koster visited the Task Force Barker TOC. By this time a ninety body count had been reported and logged by Task Force Barker.

On the afternoon, sometime between 1500 and 1645 hours, MG Koster was flying between Quang Ngai and Chu Lai when he was monitoring the radio net of Task Force Barker. He heard a discussion between one of the subordinate commanders and an individual that he thought was LTC Barker about instructions that had been given to the ground commander to return to My Lai 4 for the purpose of determining the nature of non-combatant casualties. MG Koster recalls that the ground commander was giving reasons why he thought he should not go back, primarily the lateness of the hour. Actually the conversation was between Capt. Medina and Maj. Calhoun and according to Medina, Sabre 6 came on the radio push and said, "I don't want them going through that mess". MG Koster relates that he understood the primary mission of returning to My Lai was to determine the cause of non-combatant casualties. He was aware that countermanding an order of ground troops was extremely unusual and he did it only once or twice during his tenure as commanding general. He also stated that a count of twenty non-combatant deaths was extremely unusual and significant.

There are those who are prone to read something sinister into MG Koster's countermanding of Col. Henderson's order, and, in fact, if he had been aware that non-combatants had been wantonly killed it would be an important factor. However, it is believed that MG Koster was not aware of the extent of the tragedy at My Lai 4 and that he countermanded the order to protect troops under his command from possible injuries due to mines and booby traps which could result from returning to My Lai 4 at that time of day. In other words, he was acting as any commander would in the best interests of his troops. Col. Henderson indicated that MG Koster's countermanding of his order had no effect upon his carrying out the investigation. However it is certain that it precluded then and in the near future any resweep through My Lai 4, which Barker and Medina were vigorously trying to prevent.

MG Koster returned to LZ Dottie with Gen. Doleman, a visiting dignitary, at 1645 hours that afternoon and stayed for approximately an hour. During the time they visited the TOC they were briefed on the combat assault by LTC Barker. Later that evening Col. Henderson called General Koster to give him the up-to-date number of, the 20 non-combatant casualties that occurred that day during the Task Force Barker operations. MG Koster was upset by the large number of casualties and Col. Henderson promised to give him a more complete rundown at a future date.

MG Koster is positive that he advised BG Young about countermanding the order to go back and determine the cause of the civilian casualties, although BG Young did not recall that. Approximately at noon on the 17th of March BG Young conveyed to MG Koster the story of the helicopter pilot. He told Koster that a helicopter pilot who participated in the Task Force Barker operation felt that the individuals on the ground had engaged in wild and indiscriminate firing. There were some civilians in the area, and he was concerned for their safety. The pilot had landed and had an argument of some sorts with an officer, which caused a gunship to land to make an evacuation of the Vietnamese civilians who were in danger. He had seen some bodies, but BG Young did not recall the number and if they were civilian... Also there was something about the evacuation of somebody to the Quang Ngai Hospital. MG Koster knew that he connected the report of the helicopter pilot with his countermanding of the order, and he directed BG Young to make an investigation. The whole purpose of the investigation was to establish first of all if wild firing and that sort of thing had in effect caused civilian casualties. He didn't set any time limit on the investigation but thought he would be able to receive some information back the next day. This was to be a full-fledged commander's inquiry.[68]

On the 18th MG Koster visited LZ Dottie from 1345 to 1420 because he wanted to talk to Barker firsthand to find out what his story was. LTC Barker was commander of the Task Force and was in charge of the operation and knew best what they had done on the ground. Barker and Calhoun had been in the area most of the day and Barker assured him there had been enemy contact and that the troops had in fact conducted themselves properly.

These two affirmations, enemy contact and no indiscriminate firing, were the lynchpin of Barker's cover-up reporting and the two points were constantly hammered home by Barker and Medina when talking to Koster and Henderson. In order to kill VC there had to be a firefight and because there were hundreds of civilian casualties observed by the aviators the number of VC KIA had to be substantive, i.e. 128. They kept the number of non-combatant casualties at twenty as falsely reported by Medina to Koster. To substantiate their claim of no indiscriminate firing they reported that the civilian casualties resulted from artillery and gunship fires, not small arms. It is amazing how well this quickly engineered scenario held up.

On the 18th, BG Young conveyed to him the results of Col. Henderson's interview with the pilot in question. The gist of the story was that Col. Henderson talked to the pilot for some time. He felt the pilot was an excitable young man, who had seen troops do some firing, and had seen civilians some place in front of him, and was concerned about the safety of the civilians, and felt that they should be removed from the area. Although he had seen some bodies, he hadn't seen any shooting as such, and he imagined a great deal more was going on than what had actually taken place.

On the morning of 20 March Col. Henderson saw MG Koster to relate to him the results of his investigation. There were only two of them in the office. Col. Henderson states the first thing he did was to discuss the 3 x 5 card which had been provided by LTC Barker indicating how they were killed. He then related to MG Koster the helicopter pilot's allegations, subsequently gave him a full explanation of exactly what Col. Henderson had done and to whom he had spoken and what he had received from those individuals. Col. Henderson advised MG Koster that Warrant Officer Thompson was the only one who saw something unusual and he relayed the impression that the warrant officer was confused and emotional and that the allegations were exaggerated out of proportion. In summary, he told MG Koster that the warrant officer's report could not be substantiated.

MG Koster felt that Col. Henderson's investigation was satisfactory. Col. Henderson states that his conversation with MG Koster lasted twenty to thirty minutes. If MG Koster had probed any of the testimony of Col. Henderson he would have found it to be shallow and inconclusive. If he had asked, for example, did you talk with each of the enlisted men separately and what did the squad leaders or the platoon sergeants say, he would have found out that Col. Henderson talked to no one separately and could not identify what the squad leaders or platoon sergeants or fire team leaders had said. Col. Henderson was not certain what platoon the men were from or where they had been in My Lai in relation to where the civilian bodies may or may not have been found. When Col. Henderson said he talked to all the pilots a simple probative question as to what pilot, what ship was he flying, what was his assignment, and how long was he over My Lai would have busted that statement. MG Koster did not probe in depth and accepted Col. Henderson's conclusions on faith.

At 161425Z COMUSMACV sent a congratulatory TWX to the Commanding General, Americal Division, congratulating the officers and men of C/1-20 Inf and B/4-3 Inf for outstanding action on 16 March northeast of Quang Ngai. This congratulatory TWX was forwarded by MG Koster to the commanding officer, 11th Brigade and the commanding officer, 123rd Aviation Battalion on 19 March. LTC Holladay recalls receiving it and he felt it was a bone to keep them quiet. Many of the combat troops in C/1-20 have also referred to the COMUSMACV message. SP/5 A. Flores[70] stated "When we got the citation … to me that was a cover-up." This message was probably brought to the attention of MG Koster the morning of the 17th, either shortly before or after MG Koster had received it BG Young reported to him on the allegations of the helicopter pilot. The message was forwarded from division late on the 19th. The congratulatory message from COMUSMACV, one of only a few received by the Americal Division, gave MG Koster and his staff the opportunity to review their reports to higher headquarters and to insure that these were factual. If they had reviewed the log and the spot reports for that day it would have become obvious that no non-combatant casualties were reported to higher headquarters.

The congratulatory TWX and the two positive newspaper articles gave the Charlie Company assault an aura of respectability when in reality it was a pointless slaughter.

After MG Koster's discussion with Col. Henderson he obviously became very concerned about non-combatants deaths. Within a few days he put out the 24 March letter subject: "Safeguarding of All Non-combatants"[78], which told his commanders they had to be particularly careful in their actions in and around inhabited villages. There is no question that the operation of Task Force Barker influenced the writing of this memorandum. Although MG Koster feels this memorandum was written by someone on his staff and that he signed it, neither BG Young, Col. Parson or LTC Balmer recall seeing the memorandum. LTC Balmer states that he does not recall drafting the memorandum personally or having it done anywhere in the G-3 offices of the TOC. LTC Balmer notes that the office symbol on the letter was the CG's office and he presumed it was typed in that office. It is extremely troubling to note that Col. Parson, the chief of staff, who should know what is going on in the whole division much less in his own office and that of the CG, is unable to remember the letter or anything associated with it. The lack of recall and understanding of Col. Parson and his staff contributes toward the difficulty in sorting out the extent of knowledge at the division headquarters concerning the operations at My Lai 4.

Koster's letter of 24 March specifically emphasized: discriminate use of fire power in vicinity of built-up areas: safeguards against the needless destruction of private property; and a civilian control plan for all ground operations in built-up areas suspected of housing non-combatants. Analysis of the 24 March letter to all commanders is quite interesting because either by coincidence or through knowledge this letter closely parallels that which occurred at My Lai 4.

MG Koster relates that the next factor involving the Task Force Barker Operation of 16 March 1968 which came to his attention was some VC propaganda. He feels reasonably certain that his first exposure to the propaganda was in his office and he believes that everyone is familiar with that particular document. Although in previous testimony MG Koster seems to recall not only the VC propaganda but a complaint coming through the district chief, he later believes that it was only VC propaganda that caused him to reopen the case. The type of accusations made in the propaganda leaflets were not particularly unusual, but when related to the helicopter pilot's report, further investigation appeared to be warranted to assure that firepower had not been over-utilized by the attacking troops. Somehow or other MG Koster learned that the GVN authorities were looking into the 16 March operation. He wasn't sure what they might develop or what they might conclude. In his own words he "felt that it would be desirable for us to document the statements we had and let the US troops say what they had done in this particular area, so that if anything further did develop on this we wouldn't be scurrying around trying to locate people and this sort of thing. That we'd have something that we say yes, we had an investigation here with the conclusions and here is supporting testimony." In other words, the purpose of a new investigation would be to document what had taken place as well as to see what the Vietnamese turned up. MG Koster felt that Col. Henderson's first initial investigation was satisfactory and that only further area of investigation that was left was in the Vietnamese channels. Therefore, MG Koster directed, through BG Young for Col. Henderson to put the results of the initial investigation in writing. MG Koster expected "Col. Henderson to get the statements from the individuals he had previously interrogated when he had started his interrogation had been regarding over-utilization of firepower but that what he had ascertained from them ended up confirming that the casualties that had been taken that day had been unavoidable. How, I can't explain it any better that that." In other words, MG Koster expected the documentation provided by Col. Henderson to include generally what he had found from these people verbally on the first go around.[68]

Col. Henderson received MG Koster's orders to conduct a formal investigation again through BG Young. Col. Henderson gave the investigative task to LTC Barker who upon the dissolution of Task Force Barker had become the executive officer of the 11th Brigade. Col. Henderson remembers that LTC Barker completed his investigation prior to Barker's R&R which has been established to have been between 18 April and 4 May. Although MG Koster puts no date upon his receipt of this investigation, it was probably sometime between the 10th and 26th of May. MG Koster states that he did receive a report back from Col. Henderson. "I don't remember it in detail other than it concluded that there were twenty civilian casualties that had been unavoidable or had been caused by those things in a combat action. He had attached statements from several individuals ... I think they were (these statements) probably some of each (written or typed), including company commanders, platoon leaders, aviators, artillerymen, but it didn't appear to me that he had not made a cross-section survey of the people who would have been involved in the operation. "MG Koster said that there were in excess of ten statements and probably less than thirty. He specifically recalled that the two company commanders, Capts. Medina and Michles, had made statements. He understands that Capt. Medina testified that he never made a signed statement. He is also aware of the fact that there has been no evidence in the Peers Investigation that anybody signed a statement. MG Koster had both BG Young and Col. Parson read the document. He doesn't know who else read it since he did not direct anyone else. As to the disposition of the formal report, MG Koster says, "It seems to me that BG Young had seen it before I did. Actually I know that both he and Col. Parson read it and we discussed it some and I said, this has supplied my reason for having obtained it and we will put it in a file and I handed it to Col. Parson for the file. I think I had it around for a few days. It wasn't all just motion."[68]

MG Koster appeared very positive as was Col. Henderson that he had received a formal report of investigation. It is believed that this report definitely existed. It can be surmised that the chief of staff, Col. Parson, who denies any knowledge of such a report, had it filed and this is the report LTC Brannen refers to having been found by LTC Lowder in the files of the G-1 Section, Americal Division in May of 1969. The only persons involved in the My Lai reports of investigation at division headquarters were MG Koster, BG Young and Col. Parson and as far as that goes, both BG Young and Col. Parson deny involvement. It is a fact that MG Koster did not request his very extensive staff of experts who existed to assist in such matters to look into the My Lai 4 operation. The inspector general, staff judge advocate, provost marshal, G-2, G-3, and G-5, as will be shown subsequently, were not brought into play. In fact, MG Koster and Col. Henderson agree that he discussed this matter with Col. Henderson on only one occasion on 20 March 1968. MG Koster not only did not use his staff but he personally did not get involved with any of the command chain in the division concerning this matter with the exception of 18th March visit to LTC Barker and the 20th March discussion with Col. Henderson.

Subsequent to his receipt of the formal report and prior to having it filed MG Koster "…specifically went to visit both LTC Khien, the province chief, and Col. Toan, the 2nd ARVN Division commander, to see if they had anything that they brought to light that we didn't have…. I wanted to see for sure what Khien and Toan felt about this, what their reaction was and what they were doing about it and all. That we had no report of their finding anything to see if anything had turned up and I went one morning to Province Headquarters and 2nd Division Headquarters for this purpose and this purpose alone. … I found that they had not found anything as of that date. Neither of them put any credence in this information that had originated from the VC source, that they would let me know if they had found anything more." LTC Pho, G-2, 2nd ARVN Division, remembers being called into a meeting held by the Commanding General, 2nd ARVN Division, with MG Koster, the senior advisor, and the aide of MG Koster. There were a number of other American officers present also, however, LTC Pho could not recall any specific person. LTC Pho was asked to fetch his memorandum concerning the VC propaganda and a report dated 11 April 1968 from the Son Tinh District Chief to the Quang Ngai Province Chief. This he did and those persons assembled discussed the matter for about five minutes.

MG Koster was familiar with the Task Force Barker 16 March operation. He overflew the area in the morning, monitored the radio net in the afternoon, countermanded an order, visited the LZ Dottie TOC twice on the 16th, had an extended conversation with LTC Barker on the 18th, received oral and written reports from Col. Henderson, was privy to Barker's Combat Action Report, saw Capt. Rodriguez' report of alleged atrocities, read the VC propaganda leaflet, visited both the 2nd ARVN Division and Quang Ngai Province headquarters, and read and had filed the comprehensive report written by Barker and endorsed by Henderson. This was an unusual amount of time for a busy division commander to spend on a single battalion operation. Yet, his efforts were too inadequate to determine the facts which were being obfuscated by Medina and Barker. After 20 March he failed to talk to any member at the 11th Brigade concerning the incident. Congressman Samuel S. Stratton on the House floor called attention to MG Koster's "incredible mismanagement of his command".[114]

BG George H. Young, the Assistant Division Commander for Maneuver, did not fly over the area of operations on 16 March. The first information he had concerning the operation was at the briefing that evening. After the briefing he stated he was surprised and disappointed by the fact that they had captured very few weapons … and that the division commander was also surprised by that fact. It is generally agreed that Col. Holladay and Maj. Watke came to BG Young about 0730 the morning of the 17th and reported the helicopter pilot's allegations. Although they both stated that Maj. Watke briefed him in depth on this incident, BG Young remembers concern for only two reasons: first, the ground forces were not carrying out their orders concerning the safeguarding non-combatants and second, that American troops might be firing on other American troops. This incident was reported to MG Koster by BG Young about noon of the 17th. MG Koster directed that an investigation be made. BG Young remembers that the information he passed on to Col. Henderson was to investigate the allegations that US Forces were firing into non-combatants. It was his understanding that this was primary thrust here.

He does not remember MG Koster ever discussing with him the countermanding of orders which had directed C/1/20 to return to My Lai 4 and make a count of civilian casualties by age and sex and how they were killed. He visited LZ Dottie between 1430 and 1445 hours on 17 March, however he does not recall what happened on that visit.

BG Young held a meeting at 0910, 18 March with LTC Barker, Col. Henderson, LTC Holladay, Maj. Watke and himself in LTC Barker's trailer at LZ Dottie to inform Col. Henderson to conduct the investigation into the two allegations. The meeting lasted five or ten minutes. Young does not remember telling Henderson to have the investigation in writing nor does he remember telling him to follow Article 15-6 but he did expect him to submit it in writing and that there would be substantial evidence to support his findings. He did not specify obvious details in the conduct of the investigation nor did he offer any support from division headquarters.[66]

BG Young admits the deep concern of MG Koster and that MG Koster had informed him this was a matter of urgency. Although BG Young found out about the situation at 0730 on the 17th and informed MG Koster about noon on the 17th, he didn't get around to conveying the orders to investigate to the brigade commander until 0910 on the 18th. Although there are many things an assistant division commander has to do in a division involved in a counterinsurgency environment in Vietnam, it appears that had this matter been of great importance in BG Young's mind and had there been a sense of urgency, that the meeting which was held to convey the orders to investigate would not have been postponed until the morning of 18 March.

Once the investigation was initiated, BG Young states, "I honestly and truthfully believe that I did my best to follow up on the investigation. I questioned Col. Henderson. I determined what progress he was making. He reported to me as I have indicated here and on each occasion to the best of my recollection I informed MG Koster that I had turned that over to Col. Henderson and tried to keep him posted on what progress was being made." This is in consonance with Col. Henderson who says that he constantly kept BG Young informed concerning the conduct of his investigation.

BG Young who remembered very little also corroborated in part Col. Henderson's testimony concerning the written follow-up to his oral report. He does not ever remember seeing the written report, but believes it was submitted several days after the oral report.

BG Young cannot tie the commanding general's 24 March memorandum, Safeguarding of Non-combatants, to the 16 March operation. He did not remember seeing the Task Force Barker Combat Operations Report, dated 28 March 1968, and he never saw the District Chief's memorandum concerning the 16 March operation. However, he had been informed by MACV personnel that there had been a significant number of Vietnamese alleged to have been killed northeast of Quang Ngai city. He did not report this fact to the Division G-2 but reported it to the division commander. He does not remember discussing MG Koster's visit with Col. Toan nor does he ever remember seeing VC propaganda or having a discussion on it.

It appears that BG Young's ability to recall has been impaired or that MG Koster excluded him from many follow-up actions concerning the 16 March operation. This is contrary to MG Koster's remembrances.

The General Staff
Lieutenant Colonel Tommy P. Trexler, the Assistant Chief of Staff, Intelligence (G-2) recalled the Task Force Barker Operation in My Lai 4 on 16 March and was aware of the results of the operation where 128 VC were killed, three weapons were captured and two friendlies were killed in action. He was not aware of twenty non-combatant casualties and he feels that he should have been aware of them if there were so many. He remembers the only unusual part of the operation was the discussion he had with BG Young a few days after the operation when BG Young stated he felt the operation had gone beyond what they should have done with respect to destruction. LTC Trexler presumed BG Young meant burning houses and killing animals but nothing specific was said that he could remember. Non-combatant casualties were not mentioned to his knowledge. He knows BG Young was concerned about it.

LTC Trexler recalls planning for the 16 March operation although he does not recall any operational intelligence because this operation was conducted in the 2nd ARVN Division area. His intelligence was not as good as it would have been if the operation were conducted in the Americal Division area.[80]

LTC Trexler stated that he had under him a Military Intelligence Detachment of forty personnel and about fifteen people in the G-2 Section. If these people had heard any rumors about war crimes he would have expected them to report to him. That no one reported any rumors about the My Lai 4 operation is almost unbelievable. The mass killings at My Lai 4 were known to Vietnamese authorities and rumors must have abounded. LTC Trexler related that there was no VC propaganda reported to the division by the liaison officer in 2nd ARVN Division area in Quang Ngai. In contrast to LTC Trexler's statement, LTC Blackledge, 11th Brigade S-2, recalls seeing two VC documents which he thought had been obtained by Trexler's military intelligence attachment, and which were distributed through intelligence channels to division headquarters as well as to the brigade.

As a principal staff officer whose responsibility was knowledge of VC activities in the general area, who had working for him a large military intelligence section as well as Vietnamese informants throughout the region and who had responsibility for close liaison and the exchange of information between province and ARVN officials it seems improbable that Col. Trexler would have heard nothing concerning the Task Force Barker Operation or he himself would not have received any of the subsequent VC propaganda. LTC Trexler's statements are refuted by Chaplain Lewis.

Lieutenant Colonel Jesmond D. Balmer, the Assistant Chief of Staff for Operations, (G-3) had been on leave for the week prior to 16 March and was not familiar with the planning of the operation. He first became aware of it when the acting G-3, Maj. William D. Kelly, briefed him. LTC Balmer stated that the body count of 128 was the highest for the 11th Brigade that he could remember while he was there. He also stated that there were not very many large body counts in the 11th Brigade. He did not receive any information about civilian casualties. Neither MG Koster nor BG Young called the civilian casualties to his attention. He cannot remember any operation with more than one of two Vietnamese non-combatant casualties.[81]

LTC Balmer stated that an artillery incident which killed civilians would be given on a spot report. He also stated that division monitored artillery investigations. LTC Balmer stated that infantry incidents were investigated by the brigades and that he did not maintain a suspense file in the G-3 section. He testified that they just did not deal with civilian casualties clearly identified as non-combatants even though it was required by a November 1967 MACV Directive. He could not recall instructions on rules of engagement of non-combatant casualties. Non-combatant deaths were put in spot reports and civilian casualties had operational significance because they had a direct relationship to the operations.

LTC Balmer was not aware of an investigation nor had he heard of the My Lai incident until early August 1969. Yet, the military history section shortly after the Task Force Barker assault requested that the 11th Brigade submit a Combat Activity Report for Charlie Company's activities on 16 March 1968. Why Charlie Company and not Task Force Barker? Col. Henderson claims he never saw the request and had no idea why it had been reported. Notwithstanding, LTC Barker shortstopped the requirement and personally prepared the report, submitting it on 28 March. This was another important step taken by Barker in his cover-up of My Lai 4. He again described the incident as a combat action against enemy resistance where "The enemy suffered heavily." Those suffering were only civilian non-combatants.

It is obvious that the procedures of the G-3 Section of Americal Division were remiss by not establishing an SOP for the investigation of incidents involving the killing or wounding of non-combatants during combat operations. Not only did the G-3 not direct such investigations but he did not maintain a suspense file for investigations being performed by the brigades. LTC Balmer denies any knowledge whatsoever concerning the Task Force Barker operation at My Lai 4. His statements are refuted by Chaplain Lewis.

The Americal Division log for 16 March does not indicate that any civilian non-combatant casualties resulting from Task Force Barker operations were reported to higher headquarters.

Lieutenant Colonel Charles Anistranski, the Assistant Chief of Staff, Civil Affairs, (G-5) from November 1967 until July 1968. With respect to the March 16th Task Force Barker Operation LTC Anistranski heard that an investigation was being conducted but not from anyone within the division. It was hearsay.

LTC Anistranski stated[82] that "I can recall LTC Lewis mentioning something about murders or something like that, people being killed, LTC Lewis and I were pretty close. I listened to LTC Lewis closely because he usually had gotten some good information from the troops." So LTC Anistranski, as a result of his discussion with LTC Lewis visited the 11th Brigade. His visit was prompted by an allegation that some women or children or perhaps non-combatants had been killed unnecessarily. He went down to brigade while the operation was ongoing and spoke to Col. Henderson. Col. Henderson said it was another skirmish they had had and that they had a good operation going on in that area. He dropped it right there and didn't interfere with the commander's prerogative, that prerogative being the deployment of troops.

No one else at division told him anything about the operation. In his opinion, if anyone knew what happened down there, it would be BG Young. He often flew with BG Young and he never mentioned anything about it. The VC propaganda never came to his attention. He went down to Quang Ngai City every Friday to visit with Mr. May and would present the divisions side of many of the issues that were going on in the area – and nothing was said to him about non-combatant casualties.

LTC Anistranski said he inquired about this operation with Capt. Donald J. Keshel, the Brigade S-5. Capt. Keshel said if he wanted the information he would have to talk to the brigade commander, and, the brigade commander had already given him an answer. So, he dropped out of the picture.

LTC Anistranski says that at this time, at Chu Lai, in the Spring of 1968 the name of Lt. Calley and Sgt. Mitchell were mentioned in or around division headquarters by the GI's.

Capt. Keshel, the 11ᵗʰ Brigade S-5, said that he heard rumors about the My Lai 4 operation a week after the operation. He specifically heard about it from LTC Anistranski probably on the weekend of 29 or 30 March. LTC Anistranski told him that Task Force Barker and 11ᵗʰ Brigade were in serious trouble because of what's going on in Task Force Barker area. LTC Anistranski said that the Vietnamese at province were launching an investigation into it because of what they were upset about. Capt. Keshel asked LTC Anistranski what he meant and the G-5 said in a loud voice while pointing his finger at Capt. Keshel "Don't worry about it, captain. It is being taken care of. I've got it all here (tapping a folder on his desk)." Because of this Capt. Keshel thought that both division headquarters and LTC Anistranski knew about My Lai 4.[83]

In May 1968 Capt. Keshel asked LTC Barker if during the operation his people had killed civilians and he mentioned the conversation he had had with LTC Anistranski. LTC Barker looked shocked and said "Anistranski is crazy. He had better watch what he says or he is going to get into trouble."

When Col. Henderson was asked if the division staff questioned him about the My Lai 4 operation in a formal or informal manner? He replied, he had no knowledge of any member of the division staff, other than BG Young, ever discussing this with him.

Lieutenant Colonel John L. Holladay, the CO, 123ʳᵈ Aviation Battalion and Aviation Officer meeting with BG Young about 0730 hours on 17 March has previously been discussed. LTC Holladay states that in the normal course of keeping the chief of staff informed that he related the incident to Col. Parson after the evening briefing on 17 March. LTC Holladay cannot understand at this time why Col. Parson cannot recall this conversation because he felt that he presented the information about the incident as being significant. On the morning of 18 March he participated in BG Young's meeting. The next thing LTC Holladay recalls about the My Lai 4 incident was the receipt of a congratulatory message about 19 March from MG Koster which was a retransmission from Gen. Westmoreland. He felt that this message was a bone given to keep them quiet.

Holladay next recalls[65] Col. Parson showing him a document regarding an investigation into this incident when he was in the chief of staff's office. He stated that Col. Parson was showing it to him as though he might be thinking of saying, "Here, do you want to see something?". He believes that it was close to the time of the incident when he saw the document but in questioning he identified the 24 April report as the one he saw. LTC Holladay stated that he indicated to Col. Parson, with a profanity, that he did not accept the report since it did not address Maj. Watke's allegations. Col. Parson seemed to agree with him, but he does not remember Col. Parson saying any words to him. LTC Holladay does not recall after 18 March ever discussing the story Maj. Watke had told him by questioning his aviators about their observations.

The Special Staff
Lieutenant Colonel Francis R. Lewis, the Division Chaplain was familiar with the 16 March 1968 operation of Task Force Barker. He first heard about the operation at the evening briefing on 16 March and recalls that a body count of 128 and the capture of three weapons were mentioned. There was a murmur that arose and he thinks LTC Anistranski made a remark "All but four were women and children." He remembers that no briefer mentioned civilian casualties at the evening briefing. LTC Lewis next recalled hearing about the My Lai 4 incident when Capt. Cresswell, one of his chaplains, visited his office the next day on 17 March 1968 and reported a conversation with a warrant officer who had flown in the My Lai operation. The warrant officer reported that there was unnecessary killing of civilians at My Lai. No numbers were listed. Later Chaplain Cresswell introduced WO Thompson to LTC Lewis at the club and Lewis assured Thompson that an investigation was being conducted.

LTC Lewis kept a journal of his activities and he remembers his journal states that he went to see the G-2 and G-3 that day.[67] Lewis saw both LTC Balmer and LTC Trexler he told them what Capt. Cresswell had told him. LTC Balmer said he had heard same thing that LTC Lewis had heard about this operation and said it would be looked into. LTC Lewis mentioned to LTC Balmer and LTC Trexler that there were unnecessary shootings and also mentioned about a soldier shooting the civilians. LTC Lewis feels that both understood what he was talking about immediately and he feels that it was not discussed in detail because it was their business to know it. He does not feel that he got a brush-off.

LTC Lewis discussed the incident several times with the chief of staff, Col. Parson. Col. Parson on these occasions gave him indications that the matter was being investigated. At division no one talked about it, no one told him not to talk about it but he got impressions from the chief of staff that it was not to be bantered about. The G-5, LTC Anistranski, got into the act whenever non-combatants were involved, yet he never briefed about this incident as he did other incidents.

Capt. Cresswell raised the question about the My Lai operation about five or six times. LTC Lewis thinks that Capt. Cresswell asked about the investigation so much because WO Thompson was not satisfied with what he was told. Because of Capt. Cresswell's constant inquiries he saw the chief of staff on several occasions was assured that the matter was being taking care of and he was not to make a big deal out of it.

LTC Lewis spoke to LTC Barker about this matter three to six weeks after the incident. LTC Barker said he had made a report or was going to make a report and that the people on the ground said the civilians had been killed in the course of combat operations. LTC Lewis feels that Barker told him he had questioned the company commanders. Chaplain Lewis had confidence in LTC Barker as a person so he believed his report. LTC Lewis told Capt. Cresswell that the matter had been investigated. He heard no other information about My Lai 4 from any of his chaplains or from the missionary in Quang Ngai.

The four magic words were "It is under investigation". Capt. Medina told his company; Col. Parson told LTC Lewis; Chaplain Cresswell told WO Thompson; and Maj. Watke told his aero scouts. Although Col. Henderson's commander's inquiry (investigation) was completed by 20 March, those magic words kept the lid on the division's many officers and enlisted men for months. However, most of the staffs at division, brigade and battalion headquarters said they were unaware of any investigation. It is interesting fact of military behavior that when subordinates are told that a matter is being investigated this normally satisfies them because they have faith in the integrity of their superiors and in the military system.

Major Robert F. Comeau, the Deputy Staff Judge Advocate, joined the 11th Brigade in August 1966 in Hawaii, and was the Brigade Staff Judge Advocate. He went to Vietnam with the Brigade in December 1967 and was immediately assigned as deputy division staff judge advocate. Maj. Comeau related several of the crimes and atrocities originating within the Americal Division in order to indicate what actions had been taken. Most of these were formally investigated.

Maj. Comeau stated that almost all war crimes are crimes under the Uniform Code of Military Justice and can be prosecuted under the code. He does not know of any investigation in Vietnam that started out initially as a war crime. He stated that war crimes all begin with a report of alleged incident and not as an alleged war crime. He felt that if an incident is reported to the Provost Marshal and through appropriate command levels, even if it is not reported as a war crime, it fulfills the requirement of MACV Directive 20-4.

It was Maj. Comeau's interpretation that the responsibility for initiating an investigation under MACV Directive 20-4 did not rest with 11th Brigade but with division headquarters. He didn't think it would be unreasonable for a division commander or a commander with a staff judge advocate or his staff to make a report to the MACV staff judge advocate. It was Maj. Comeau's judgment that if a combat operation caused the deaths of innocent civilians it could be a war crime if the civilians were intentionally killed. He stated that if twenty innocent civilians were killed it would require some type of investigation. Maj. Comeau was shown the 24 April report, and stated on its face it was inadequate in his mind because it leaves questions open and probably needs further investigation. When shown WO Thompsons' allegations he stated that they were serious enough to warrant an investigation.[85]

Maj. Comeau felt a subordinate making an investigation would be relieved of the responsibility if the investigation was accepted by higher headquarters without comment. But a person making a report of investigation would not be relieved of his responsibility if statements contained intentional incorrect facts or if person omitted facts willfully. Maj. Comeau concluded by agreeing that the adequacy or inadequacy of investigation is in the eyes and mind of the reviewer. It was concluded that an officer in the field has the responsibility to report and the senior command has the responsibility to investigate and that any directive to investigate under MACV Directive 20-4 should have come down through the Americal Division.

Lieutenant Colonel James H. Hetherly, the Inspector General, stated he had no recall of the incident of 16 March 1968. Further, he was not asked to investigate this incident nor did he hear of anyone investigating.[86]

Lieutenant Colonel Warren J. Lucas, the Provost Marshal, said that he did not have any report of the incident at My Lai 4 and felt that if such an incident occurred on 16 March 1968 as alleged that he would have been told to check into it. During the two weeks period subsequent to 16 March he visited the 11th Brigade and did not hear anything from anyone that anything unusual had happened on the Task Force Barker assault. LTC Lucas felt that if there were rumors going throughout the military police company about assaults, war crimes or common law crimes he would have expected to have heard about them.[87]

Chief of Staff
Colonel Nels A. Parson[79], who held the position in the Americal Division from 2 February 1968 through May 1968 stated he became aware of the deaths associated with the 16 March operation but he is not sure when that was unless it was the 24 April report. He is certain he learned of them while still in Vietnam. He stated that he saw a report or reports but he cannot remember what he saw. Whatever the report was, it resolved the issue. He thinks it was more than one report and didn't like to limit it only to one. He had no recollection of oral discussions. He recalls that he was informed that a helicopter pilot reported that many civilians had been killed unnecessarily. However, he doesn't remember who told him this. He also recalls Col. Henderson conducting an investigation into this matter and submitting a written report. He believes that he read that report but what he read didn't make him believe anything had happened. He didn't recall ever attending a staff briefing concerning the My Lai operation either before 16 March 1968 or after. The My Lai incident was just not highlighted in his mind. He didn't remember the incident being discussed with him by Chaplain Lewis. He does remember a letter that had been written by a Vietnamese official about the incident but he is not sure what it said and he is sure that he gave it to MG Koster. LTC Holladay, states that he informed the Chief of Staff, Col. Parson, about the incident after the evening briefing at 1700 on the 17th of March. He also recalls Col. Parson close to the time of the incident showing him a document regarding an investigation into the incident. LTC (Chaplain) Lewis states[67] that he discussed the My Lai incident several times with the chief of staff, but it was not on official business.

Specialist Hill, secretary to Col. Parson, first remembers[76] the My Lai incident when Col Holladay and a warrant officer pilot came to visit the division headquarters and wanted to see MG Koster. It was about two days after a very high body count figure was posted on Col. Parson's chart. LTC Holladay went to see Col. Parson with this man before he went to see MG Koster. Hill then recalls a flap caused by some Vietnamese civilian who claimed that a large number of innocent civilians had been killed as a result of an operation of Task Force Barker. This was one or two weeks after LTC Holladay had come in with the warrant officer. This resulted in a large number of telephone calls between Col. Parson and LTC Guinn, Maj. Gavin and Mr. May who were the liaison with the 2nd ARVN Division. After this a US Army captain, he believes it was Capt. Rodriguez, brought a report concerning a complaint that had been made by a Vietnamese civilian to the Command Headquarters and gave it to Col. Parson. About 24 April Col. Henderson gave a report to Col. Parson. Hill goes on to say that Col. Parson gave a short suspense date to Col. Henderson for a report and when he received Col. Henderson's report it was considered inadequate. MG Koster thought in his discussion with BG Young that Col. Parson was present. MG Koster also states that Col. Parson read the 24 April report of Col. Henderson's and MG Koster knows that both BG Young and Col. Parson read the formal report and after it was discussed and he handed it to Col. Parson for the file.

There is strong evidence that Col. Parson was intimately involved in the follow-up actions resulting from the 16 March Task Force Barker Operation. His inability to recall such serious allegations and papers of such vital import to the American Division cannot be comprehended. In addition, Col. Parson, as chief of staff, was responsible to the commanding general to insure that his staff operated effectively in support of the commanding general. He had the responsibility to follow up on allegations of this sort and to insure that the investigative capabilities of the division staff were utilized. He failed to do this. Gen. Peers was harsh concerning Col. Parson's performance writing "Personally, I found his attitude towards his position as division chief of staff to be astounding."[1]

Had Col. Parsons used any of his available staff to either investigate or to assist Col. Henderson they would have certainly quickly determined that the reports from LTC Barker and Capt. Medina were misleading. There was no enemy resistance. There was no artillery, tactical air or gunship requests for support. The report of sixty-nine enemy killed in an open field was false. Charlie Company had no casualties resulting from enemy action yet eliminated ninety VC. Had anyone further interrogated the pilots flying on 16 March they would have learned that they saw many dead non-combatants. Col. Parson, Gen. Koster's right-hand man, should have galvanized his staff into action, supported Henderson in his investigation and followed-up on the many reports he received. He dropped the ball.

That the American Division staff did not actively participate in the investigation of WO Thompson's allegations was a major failure preventing the atrocities from coming to light in Vietnam. The question is why? MG Koster initially kept WO Thompson's report close hold but later stated he thought his staff would participate. Interestingly the division, brigade and task force commanders all did not involve their staffs.

Summary of Division Headquarters Actions

The response of the American Division headquarters to the reports of non-combatant casualties at My Lai 4 is intriguing. MG Koster immediately ordered an investigation on 17 March. Subsequently, when the Vietnamese propaganda surfaced he directed an in-depth substantiated follow-on investigation. Unfortunately BG Young, upon Col. Henderson's advice, allowed LTC Barker to conduct the in-depth investigation. Col. Henderson later admitted that it never occurred to him that Barker was investigating his own operation and in fact was not being truthful.

As soon as possible MG Koster conducted his own investigation, meeting with LTC Barker at LZ Dottie for about an hour on 18 March. Barker stated that he had flown over the area of conflict and assured MG Koster that the troops had conducted themselves properly. Consequently when Col. Henderson made his oral report on 20 March, which paralleled Barker's previous comments, MG Koster felt the report was satisfactory.

Initially MG Koster kept WO Thompson's allegations close hold within the command section keeping both BG Young and Col. Parson informed, although they both state they recalled little if any, of the information concerning the incident.

The chief of staff inexplicably did not involve his general staff in any follow-up actions. The G-2, G-3 and G-5 all claim they knew nothing of the non-combatant casualties, notwithstanding the fact that LTC (Chaplain) Lewis informed them according to his detailed notes which he kept. The G-2 who had close liaison ties with the Vietnamese unbelievably stated he had no knowledge of the VC propaganda although the leaflet obtained by his military intelligence detachment, was forwarded to the division by the 11th Brigade through intelligence channels. The G-3 had no system to record non-combatant casualties nor knowledge of the requirement to report them. The G-5 knew civilians had been killed but never briefed the fact. The aviation officer, although thoroughly briefed on 17 March 1968 concerning the incident, failed to interrogate his aviators

The special staff, the staff judge advocate, provost marshal and inspector general, those officers whose duty was normally to assist and investigate such matters as occurred at My Lai 4 were never informed and were not utilized.

The American Division Headquarters command section and key general staff were all expeditiously informed that a large number of non-combatants had been killed during the Task Force Barker 16 March operation. The headquarters received several investigative reports, the Rodriguez letter and the VC propaganda leaflet, yet all, except MG Koster, saw nothing and heard nothing. The actions or lack of actions taken by the division staff concerning My Lai 4 were almost dysfunctional. After 20 March except for MG Koster's requests for Col. Henderson to investigate and his visits to the senior Vietnamese officers there were no follow-up activities by him or by division headquarters. No assistance whatsoever was provided to Col. Henderson in the conduct of his investigations. The order to investigate and Col. Henderson's follow-up actions are discussed subsequently.

INVESTIGATING THE OPERATION

General Koster, in discussing his conversation with General Young to investigate,[68] stated, "Well, some place along the line I am sure I told him to make an investigation of this, and it also seems to me that I just didn't feel that an incident like this was apt to have happened." When asked concerning the instructions he gave to General Young as to who was to conduct the investigation and what were the parameters, General Koster replied, "I'm not positive that I did anything more than tell him to investigate it. If I did, I don't recall. I certainly thought any investigation of it would have involved talking to the people on the ground and the people flying in the helicopters...The purpose of the investigation was to look into the helicopter pilot's argument with the man on the ground, his actions at the time whether the ground personnel had done the wild firing, whether they had in fact endangered somebody they shouldn't have and the inference all being, were there civilian casualties? ...I wanted to know what went on down there and all aspects of it ... First of all I wanted to establish if the wild firing and that sort of thing had in effect caused civilian casualties". To the best of his knowledge, General Koster did not set a time limit. He thought he would receive some information back the next day and had in mind a commander's inquiry.

The Order to Investigate

General Young held a meeting on 18 March at LZ Dottie with Colonel Henderson, LTC Holladay, LTC Barker, Major Watke and himself at LTC Barker's trailer.[66] This meeting was to inform Col. Henderson to conduct an investigation into two allegations: first, the ground forces were not carrying out their orders concerning non-combatants and second, that American troops might be firing on other American troops. The allegations stated by Major Watke were outlined at the meeting. General Young didn't direct Col. Henderson to personally conduct the investigation, but had no objections for him doing it. When informed, General Koster voiced no objection either. General Young does not remember telling Col. Henderson to have the investigation in writing nor does he remember telling him to follow AR 15-6. He did expect him to submit it in writing and that there would be substantial evidence to support the findings. He stated this matter was of significance and concern to him and the division commander.

Maj. Watke was asked to relate the WO pilot's story for the benefit of Col. Henderson. Watke left the meeting with the complete understanding that Col. Henderson was told to conduct an investigation concerning the unnecessary shooting, wounding and killing of civilians which was so bad that the aviators had landed on the ground in front of troops. That was the thing that really disturbed Watke, since "pilots just didn't do that". Although the interaction between the pilot and the ground troops was mentioned, Watke felt Col. Henderson was not investigating the confrontation since that matter had been settled in a meeting on the 17th.[50] Holladay recalls that General Young told Col. Henderson to investigate this and have it to him in some striking short period of time. Those were the only directions given and he felt that the directions were clear.

Col. Henderson's recollection of the meeting at LZ Dottie was entirely different from the other participants. Col. Henderson incorrectly felt strongly that he had talked to WO Thompson prior to the meeting with General Young. "Well, I know the meeting was kicked off by General Young with a very positive statement that under no circumstances am I going to have US troops firing on US troops, and he went into a sort of a philosophy discussion, but very definitely directed to myself and to Col. Barker and to Col. Holladay and if Watke was there it was directed to him too, what he wasn't going to permit. So he placed strong emphasis on the confrontation or the threat of pilots shooting at the ground troops." As far as Col. Henderson was concerned, General Young's directives at that time settled the helicopter confrontation. [53]

Col. Henderson states that General Young did not direct an investigation to take place. He felt he informed him ... "that I was initially going to take a look at this thing from a commander's viewpoint but if there were any grounds or any evidence at all to substantiate the allegations of WO Thompson that I would, then, recommend that a formal investigation be conducted. But I'm differentiating here between a formal investigation by orders as opposed to what is the responsibility of the commander. I think I'm differentiating; at least in my own mind I am."[17]

It is felt that General Koster's directive for Col. Henderson to investigate the allegations of WO Thompson which was conveyed by General Young was imprecise. No parameters were given. No detailed instructions were provided. No guidelines were cited. No assistance was offered. It was all done orally with nothing in writing. Considering the statements of General Koster and the four living members of the meeting at LZ Dottie it appears that the only item upon which there is complete agreement is that Col.

111

Henderson was instructed to investigate the unnecessary shooting, wounding and killing of civilians (non-combatants). Major Watke's and Col. Henderson's recollection was that the other area of major concern to General Young, that is, the confrontation between the helicopter pilot and some men on the ground, was settled at a meeting at LZ Dottie on 17 March.

Col. Henderson's Investigative Actions
Discussions During the Assault
Col. Henderson claims he had the following discussions in preparation for his oral report to MG Koster. While flying in his helicopter over the area of combat operations on 16 March, he saw a house burst into flames on the southwest side of My Lai 4 and saw dead non-combatant Vietnamese on the North-South trail south of the village. On the occasion of one or the other or both of these incidents he asked LTC Barker the cause(s), who replied it was the result of artillery and gunship firings. Henderson tasked him to determine how they were killed and to give him a fuller explanation. Barker provided this information to him on the 19th written on a 3 x 5 card.[53]

Henderson asked LTC Luper a question concerning the artillery prep. Although Luper could not recall a discussion about the prep it is not improbable that the brigade commander could have asked his artillery battalion commander such a question, particularly since he himself had not visually observed the artillery preparation.

On a later occasion Col. Henderson may have asked LTC Luper to check into the cause of the twenty non-combatant casualties which had been reported as killed by artillery and/or gunships.[11] LTC Luper denies this vigorously and Col. Henderson is not firm at all in his recollection. Captain Holbrook,[102] the Assistant S-2 of the 11th Brigade when asked if he had any knowledge about an investigation conducted by LTC Luper, replied Col. Henderson told LTC Luper to check into the artillery prep that was laid out that day, but he didn't know what action LTC Luper took.

Discussions with Light Observation Helicopter Pilot
At the conclusion of BG Young's 18 March meeting about 0930 hours, Maj. Watke recalls[50] that "Col. Henderson asked me to remain and I did so. He asked me about two questions, but I don't recall either question, but they were very brief. He also asked me if I would send up the pilots. I sent up three people, but I am not sure if he specified each and every one that he wanted or whether he just asked me to send up some of the crew. I sent up three people one of whom was a Mr. Thompson. And I've always in my

mind though it was the commander of the other two gunships. However, I have previously spoken to Thompson, and he indicated it was his gunner and crew chief but I don't recall that. There were three people. I recall they came to my van the previous day. I'm not sure if they were the same three people but that is what I've always thought. I didn't specifically see them go up, but as I recall they came back separately. I don't even know for a fact that all of them went in to see Col. Henderson. But they went up together. My recollection is, Mr. Thompson came back alone and briefed me on what had transpired."

LTC Luper recalls Col. Henderson talking with WO Thompson on the same day that Col. Henderson went out into the field to talk with Capt. Medina. He does not recall if the conversation with WO Thompson was before or after the conversation with Capt. Medina.

Col. Henderson's discussion with the Light Observer Helicopter Pilot, who he refers to as WO Thompson, is important. It is also an event that is not too clear,[11] since neither Henderson nor Thompson recognized each other as the party involved in the interview in Vietnam. Col. Henderson initially thought the interview with the OH-23 pilot took place in the morning of the 17th, but when prompted agreed it took place on the 18th. However, he was still confused whether it occurred before or after his meeting with BG Young. Although the timing of the interview is germane – it is the content that is of vital importance.

Col. Henderson recalls Thompson made two allegations. He observed both troops on the ground and aircraft shooting wildly, and shooting at anything and everything that moved, and that he had specifically observed a captain shoot and kill a wounded female, a woman…"One other thing I would like to add in here. He reported having observed many dead in the area. This agreed with the report I had that there were twenty civilians killed and approximately, or a figure of 128 VC killed in the area. So I related in effect what he had seen as these civilians were the VC that had been killed in the area. I did not consider that a major atrocity or any degree of an atrocity had occurred. I took it for granted the people he saw were VC, but his report implied at least they were from his viewpoint non-combatants. I did gather from him that he was speaking of non-combatants being shot. But if he saw 148 total bodies, he did not relate that to me, and I came away with the impression that he hadn't. What he, in fact had seen was VC KIA and possibly some of the twenty." [17]

"There was no doubt in my mind but what he was reporting to me that he had seen a number of civilians killed—that he had seen their bodies, I should say that. He didn't see any of them killed, except the Medina one. He was saying 'yes, civilians, but not in family groups, but all over the area.' And I figured, I got the impression that he was saying, one here, and one there."[11]

"I do not believe that WO Thompson was complaining about the total numbers out there. What he was complaining about was basically two things, one, that this captain had specifically shot this woman, and secondly, that he had marked a number of positions with smoke, expecting US forces to come over and render first aid, and that in fact US forces, apparently, now, I'm sure he told me they advanced on these positions shooting. But then when I tried to pin him down, well where was somebody actually shot, tell me exactly where someone was shot, and he kept coming back to this Medina all the time. And I got the impression that the biggest thing that WO Thompson saw out there that day, and was concerned about and was angry about and was upset about, was this captain shooting the woman. I do not recall specifically asking him to tell me how many people you saw dead out there. Frankly I don't think he knew how many he had seen dead."[53]

Henderson asked the warrant officer some questions, but at the time he was so emotional that Henderson was not sure he could get much more out of him. "I felt I had from him what I could get. The man at the time-I still feel, although after meeting-if WO Thompson was in fact the individual who made the report to me, since I have seen him subsequently, he does not appear to be exactly the same man, the young man standing in front of me was extremely upset emotionally. If it was WO Thompson who made this initial report to me, I did not again speak to that man."[17]

Col. Henderson stated in his discussions with WO Thompson that the items of the ditch with a pile of bodies; evacuation of a small child; evacuation of Vietnamese from the bunker; confrontation with a lieutenant; and a colored sergeant pointing his weapon in a ditch which contained some dead non-combatants were not discussed.

With respect to the pilots threatening the ground troops he was certain that when he finished the conversation with BG Young, that there was anything further to do about the confrontation. That issue was resolved there at that time and he didn't believe that he ever once again tied in this pilot as being the same pilot that had been talking to him. [17]

WO Thompson[49] testified that he and Colburn went to an interview either on the 17th or the 18th. However, he believes that it was the 18th because he didn't fly on the 17th of March. He was interviewed at LZ Dottie on the hill close to a water tower or similar kind of structure. He was in a covered area and seems to recall some canvas or mosquito netting in the room. "Either Colburn or Andratta went with me. I thought there was one of the gunship pilots, but I don't remember whether one of them went up there or not. Somebody waited outside and I think it was Colburn, but I'm not sure. The other individual could have been Mr. Culverhouse."

Thompson cannot identify the interviewer and he could not consider Col. Henderson to be the person who interviewed him. He did not remember talking to Col. Henderson in Vietnam.

"I told him everything that I had seen.[89] Like I said before, I can't see why I wouldn't. Everything was a lot fresher on my mind then than it is now. Actually, you know, our conversation—I can't recall what all was said. I'm not even sure it was Col. Henderson I talked to. You are asking me to go back almost two years and I can't be real specific."

WO Thompson felt the interview was between ten and twelve in the morning and lasted 20 to 30 minutes. He told the interviewer he had seen the captain shoot the Vietnamese girl and told him about the bodies in the ditch. When asked how many bodies did you tell him were in the ditch, he responded, "Between 75 and 100. There are a bunch of people there. I told him about the sergeant saying the only way he could help them was to shoot them. I told him that when I sat down over there I talked with the man who appeared to be in charge, and that I told him that I had spotted some Vietnamese kids in the bunker, and he said, "No, you're kidding and that the only way he could get them out was with a hand grenade. So I told him to just stop his men and I'd get them out of there without killing them."

Comparing Col. Henderson's recollections with WO Thompson's there is almost complete disagreement as to time of interview, as to who accompanied WO Thompson, who was present at the interview, as to length of interview and to the allegations. The most important factor is that Col. Henderson did interview the OH-23 pilot who was WO Thompson and was informed of wild shooting by the troops which resulted in a large number of non-combatant casualties.

<u>Discussions with Other Aviators</u>
At the conclusion of WO Thompson's interview Col. Henderson may have interviewed two other personnel. However, Col. Henderson[53] indicated the only individual he talked to at LZ Dottie on the morning of 18 March was

WO Thompson. He was positive he did not talk to either WO
Culverhouse or Specialist Colburn. The facts surrounding these potential
interviews are discussed subsequently.

WO Culverhouse[51] was interviewed about what he had seen at My Lai 4
shortly after the incident. On the day of questioning he was already on the
helipad at LZ Dottie and he was told by WO Thompson that someone on
top of the hill wanted to talk with him about what he had seen on 16
March. WO Thompson took him to the place of the interview and pointed
out the building to him. The only other person WO Culverhouse saw there
was Specialist Colburn.

WO Culverhouse went into the building and reported to the officer who
was seated. He told the officer about the village being on fire, the bodies
throughout the village, the large number of bodies of men, women and
children in the ditch (about seventy-five in all), the colored NCO pointing
his weapon at the ditch and the evacuation of the people from the bunker.
He said there was no movement in the ditch and remembers relating that
there was a lot of blood flowing off the bodies. He recalls this certain part
about the ditch because the officer asked him questions concerning it. The
officer also asked how he could tell that the man standing by the ditch was
an NCO. WO Culverhouse said he remembers seeing the subdued
chevrons on his arm. WO Culverhouse is quite certain he told everything.
He thought the officer was concerned at least professionally, but he does
not know who questioned him. It was either a LTC or a full colonel. WO
Culverhouse feels he would have recalled it if there was a full colonel
because it would have impressed him more. No one was in the building
when he was there and no one accompanied him into the room. He did
not see either WO Thompson or Specialist Colburn speak to the individual.
WO Culverhouse indicated that none of Col. Henderson's mannerisms, his
voice, nor his looks seemed familiar to him.

Specialist Colburn[96] stated about noon on 18 March he was by his
helicopter in the flight line at LZ Dottie when WO Thompson came down
and asked him if he would make a statement to Col. Henderson, the brigade
commander. He waited outside a dug-in sandbagged building for about ten
minutes and remembers seeing Specialist Culverhouse who was around the
area. He went down some steps into a fairly small room which had a field
table and two small chairs. He reported to a full colonel who had short hair
and wore glasses. Colburn indicated by pointing that Col. Henderson was
the individual he talked to. The interview lasted five or ten minutes. He
told him about the captain he saw shoot the women and the bodies in the
ditch. There were sixty to seventy old men and women and children in the

116

ditch who appeared to have been killed by small arms. He thought this was a "needless killing of innocent civilians." He said we did pop smoke on wounded Vietnamese and the infantry came over and killed them. He also mentioned that WO Thompson took people out of a bunker before the troops got there. The interviewer asked two questions that he can recall: could the people have been killed by artillery or not? and the number of people in the ditch?

There is no more reason to consider that Col. Henderson interviewed WO Thompson than it is to consider that he interviewed WO Culverhouse or Specialist Colburn. The only thing that links Col. Henderson to WO Thompson at all is the fact that LTC Luper saw WO Thompson at LZ Dottie in the company of Col. Henderson and a field grade aviation officer. Testimony has indicated that Maj. Watke was requested by Col. Henderson to provide him with three helicopter personnel who had seen what occurred on 16 March. There is no one that visually saw WO Thompson, WO Culverhouse and Specialist Colburn being interviewed. There is general agreement as to the date of the interviews but the time of interviews varies somewhat. There is agreement as to who brought the individuals to the interview and all three interviewed saw the other two in the vicinity while they were at the top of the hill at LZ Dottie. Both Culverhouse and Colburn recall being interviewed in a below ground sandbagged bunker and stepping down stairs to enter. This fits the description of the tactical operations center and it is possible that Culverhouse was interviewed by LTC Barker.

The questions asked by the interviewer were almost the same for WO Thompson and for Specialist Colburn. WO Thompson is certain that he was interviewed by a colonel but he cannot recognize him. WO Culverhouse is not sure whether he was interviewed by a lieutenant colonel or a colonel and cannot identify Col. Henderson as the man who interviewed him nor does he rule him out. Specialist Colburn definitely recognized Col. Henderson as the individual who interviewed him. Although what the individuals related to the interviewer varies, they all discussed the great number of non-combatant bodies in the ditch, varying from sixty to one hundred. Therefore, whether Col. Henderson interviewed one, two or three of these individuals, he was informed by these personnel of a large number (sixty or greater) of non-combatants killed at one specific location at My Lai 4. Circumstantial evidence indicates that Col. Henderson probably talked to all three.

It is emphasized that each of the three members of the 123rd Aviation Battalion in their interviews definitely asserted that they mentioned bodies in the ditch and an actual number of non-combatants killed. The testimonies of Culverhouse and Colburn add no new facts to WO Thompson's allegations, but are reinforcing. Looking at it another way, since the information provided the interviewer was generally the same concerning non-combatant deaths, if Col. Henderson did not interview WO Culverhouse and Specialist Colburn it would be an indication that his investigation was not as thorough as if he had interviewed them.

Discussion with LTC Barker
Col. Henderson recalls before he went to see Capt. Medina he talked to LTC Barker for a short period of time about the incident, and apparently the helicopter pilot's story had already been related by either Maj. Watke or Warrant Officer Thompson to Barker because he was aware of it. Barker was quite forceful in falsely informing him that there was no truth to this alleged wild shooting and that the company was heavily engaged with the enemy. Later "I informed Col. Barker that I was not satisfied. Thompson's report to me was loud and clear. I believed Thompson had seen some of the things that he had reported to me, and that Medina did not appear to know what in the hell had occurred. Barker was quite strongly opposed to moving the company back through there. I believe he told me that he himself had set down in the vicinity of My Lai 4 and that he hadn't seen any of this … However, I refused to accept his argument and told him I wanted that company to go back through there and render a report by the type; male, female, and children, how they were killed; and that they were inspected by an officer. While they were at it, they could look around in those rice paddies to see if they could pick up any weapons." [53]

Col. Henderson summarized his discussions with LTC Barker as follows: "He told me that there had been no indiscriminate killing of civilians, that although he acknowledged that some of these civilians had probably been killed by small arms fire, that he had been over that area, that he had talked to people, and that he was positive that nothing such as Warrant Officer Thompson reported had occurred. And I placed a great deal of reliance in Col. Barker. But that's my responsibility." [53]

He also talked to Col. Barker to resolve the discrepancy between the reports of twenty and twenty-eight non-combatants killed. Barker had told Medina that Col. Henderson had seen six to eight bodies, and when Medina gave his report he increased his number of twenty by six to eight and made it twenty-eight.

It is impossible to obtain LTC Barker's side of the story because he was killed on a combat mission on 13 June 1968. However, it appears from what LTC Barker supposedly said to Col. Henderson and LTC Barker's Combat Action Report which he personally wrote, that he was less than truthful concerning the operation and was attempting to cover-up. Both Col. Henderson and MG Koster relied heavily upon LTC Barker's reporting.

It appears subsequent to BG Young's meeting which terminated about 0930 hours that there was sufficient time for Col. Henderson to have had an interview with WO Thompson (and others), to have had a brief discussion with Barker and to have arrived at Medina's location in the field about 1400 hours, the time recalled by LTC Blackledge and Capt. Medina.

Discussion with Capt. Medina
Col. Henderson felt that Warrant Officer Thompson's allegations were quite serious and this is why he immediately went to the field to Capt. Medina's position.[53] On the way, the helicopter flew over My Lai 4 and Henderson observed it with field glasses, looking for anything that would support what WO Thompson had told him. He did not see any bodies. The only bodies he ever saw were two uniformed VC with weapons to the north of the village and six to eight civilian non-combatants to the south side of the village along the trail where it junctions into Highway 521.

LTC Blackledge, 11th Brigade S-2, accompanied Col. Henderson to the field when he talked to Capt. Medina on the 18th of March.[88] Col. Henderson took charge of the conversation. LTC Blackledge thought the questioning was unusual because Col. Henderson did not ask Capt. Medina about other aspects of the operation but went into civilian casualties to a considerable extent. The thrust of Col. Henderson's inquiry was to make sure the body count was valid and to make sure that troops understood the importance of not unnecessarily killing civilians. Col. Henderson was not unfriendly during questioning but it was close questioning and Capt. Medina had come back with answers in a straightforward manner.

Regarding his own activities Capt. Medina stated that he had shot a woman because of her sudden movement. He fired before he realized she was a woman. She had medical supplies with her and he called her a VC nurse.

Col. Henderson asked Capt. Medina if there were bodies in the area that he could look at and Medina said no. Henderson asked if they could go to the place where the bodies were and Capt. Medina said he would have to have one of his platoons accompany them into the area. This idea was cancelled because of the difficulty of calling a platoon to return several kilometers just prior to its evacuation. However, when asked if Col. Henderson mentioned anything to him about returning to My Lai 4, Capt. Medina replied "He did not."

Capt. Medina falsely assured Col. Henderson that no civilians had been killed by ground troops but they had been killed by artillery or gunships and denied there had been indiscriminate firing. He assured him that his platoon leaders had no knowledge of indiscriminate killing. Col. Henderson was suspicious of the 128 body count but didn't tell Medina that. He asked Medina where were the bodies, since he hadn't seen them? Capt. Medina said that there were a great number of them spread out in bushes and among trees where the gunships had taken them under fire. Others were in the defensive bunkers around the village. Col. Henderson continued to hold his suspicions and belatedly wished he had appointed an investigating office instead of handling the situation himself. "I think some of my thinking was that I had just assumed command of this brigade and that it was my brigade and dammit, I wanted to run it. I wanted to find out what in the hell was happening. I didn't yet have control, I recognized that. I know when I went out there to see Medina that I expected to relieve him, until he came back to me with this somewhat plausible explanation."[17]

When he broached the subject to Capt. Medina of the fact that there was a pilot marking wounded, Capt. Medina said that he had no knowledge that this individual was marking wounded. This signal was always reserved for marking VC. He directed all of his elements, as he dispatched them out to investigate these smoke signals, to advance cautiously because he did not want to get people killed unnecessarily.

Col. Henderson had no recollection of attempting to reconcile the report of twenty civilian casualties within the impact area of artillery or gunships and he did not inquire about the sixty-nine KIA killed by artillery fire.

Medina informed him that the number of civilian casualties was reported to him by his platoon leaders, although later Medina reported he personally had observed the civilian casualties and had received negative reports from his platoon leaders. Henderson made no attempt to inquire about wounded civilians and made no inquiry into Charlie Company casualties. He could not explain why the company had been engaged in a heavy fire fight and met strong resistance without incurring any casualties.

Capt. Medina stated in their discussion,[23] "He asked me if I was aware of any atrocities in My Lai 4. I told him no. He asked me if my people were aware of it, and he asked me if I thought my people could do such a thing, and I told him I did not think American soldiers would do such a thing. He said, 'Okay. We are going to conduct an investigation of this.' Then he called for his helicopter and left."

At the conclusion of the questioning Col. Henderson has repeatedly stated that he had no feelings that anything wrong had happened. He felt that Capt. Medina had answered all of the warrant officer's allegations. He believed Medina was on top of the situation because he unhesitantly and straightforwardly answered all of his questions. Henderson admitted it never occurred to him that Medina most probably had been informed by LTC Barker of WO Thompson's allegations prior to his visit and stated this could answer to some degree why Medina's explanations were so spontaneous.[17]

Capt. Medina while not under oath in October 1970, admitted he was not completely candid in his testimony before the Peers Inquiry. Further, when he reported to Col. Henderson that he had seen twenty to twenty-eight non-combatant casualties he purposely did not tell him they were all in one group on the north-south trail and gave him the impression they probably had been killed by artillery or gunship fires because he did not want to believe his people could have done this. Additionally, when Capt. Medina questioned his platoon leaders on the evening of 16 March they had informed him that at least 106 civilians had been killed that day.[112] These admissions greatly discredit Medina's veracity. Medina was doing his best to put a positive face on his actions at My Lai 4 and was definitely attempting to cover-up his company's out of control conduct.

Discussions with Capt. Michels and Capt. Riggs
After visiting Capt. Medina on the 18th Col. Henderson[17] believes he talked to Capt. Michles, the company commander of B Co 4/3rd Inf., and to Capt. Riggs, the company commander of A Co.3rd/1st Infantry, on the 18th. He had noticed on the early morning hours of 18 March that Alpha Company had a couple of men killed and another three wounded by a single booby trap detonation. This was of concern to him because on the 16th of March he had put out instructions that he wanted space between people when they were moving in the field. After he talked to Capt. Medina he would also have spoken to Capt. Riggs about it.

Verification of Col. Henderson's talk with Capt. Michles is difficult because the captain was killed in combat. However, LTC Luper who flew with Col. Henderson on March 18th clearly recalls the conversation that he had with Capt. Medina in the Pinkville area but does not recall Col. Henderson talking to Capt. Michles. He only recalls him talking to one company commander.

Capt. Riggs stated[92] he had no knowledge of an investigation having been conducted in Vietnam about the operation of 16 March 1968. He knows he was never questioned about it while he was in Vietnam. It is concluded that Col. Henderson did not speak to Capt. Riggs concerning the My Lai 4 operation and it is impossible to verify whether or not he spoke to Capt. Michles.

Discussions with Troops at LZ Dottie
Upon leaving Capt. Medina's field position Col. Henderson flew to LZ Dottie where he observed some of the troops from Charlie Company landing from their extraction. On 2 December 1969 Col. Henderson related what transpired.[53] "I did not go up there with the idea of really talking to these troops. I went up there to find out why my orders were countermanded – what reason for it. The men did not know me as their brigade commander, since I had just assumed command a day or two before that. I wanted them to see me. I wanted to see them. I felt that in light of not being able to sweep them back through this area, maybe I could get something out of them. I realized it was just a feather in the wind, but it was my hope that if something had gone wrong, that one of them or groups of them would have spoken up and told me what it was. I have thought of it since and I agree, psychologically it would have been a bad time. And I wouldn't expect a man to stand up and say, 'Yes, I killed a bunch of people.'"

"I'm certain that I received no oral response from the group. Looking at these men there was not a single man that was trying to avoid my eye or trying to appear if he hadn't heard me or in any way indicate to me any reluctance to say anything, it was just that no individual volunteered to say anything oral.... I talked to those men and I did not believe at that time and I still don't believe that those men were soldiers who had just come out of the area after killing a bunch of women and children."[53, 17]

He stated that he had not made any efforts to get the platoon leaders and a few of the key platoon sergeants and some of the soldiers off to the side where he might talk to them individually if he wanted to find out something.

Sgt. Buchanon, the Platoon Sergeant of the 2nd Platoon, C/1-20 Inf., recalls that he was lifted out on a Huey along with SFC. Cowan, the 1st Platoon Sergeant.[39] They went to LZ Dottie, and started towards the bunkers. Col. Henderson was walking up the path to the pad and said "Do you men feel that you conducted yourselves on this operation so the Vietnamese people can say these are our friends?" The people all hesitated, and then he asked Sgt. Buchanon, "How about you?", and 1Sgt Buchanon replied by saying "I have no comment." Buchanon stated that Col. Henderson did not question anyone further that he knew of and he gave that answer because he did not understand what was meant by the question. There were about five or six GI's in the group."

It is important to analyze what Col. Henderson wanted to believe. The only answer he obtained was "No comment"; an answer which should have alerted him. Col. Henderson looked at these men and because they didn't avert his eyes he felt that they were giving him a positive reply. In this respect Col. Henderson was very naïve. The fact of the matter was that Col. Henderson didn't expect anything because he didn't anticipate that this is what had happened. In other words, he had then and has now faith in enlisted personnel that precluded his mind from grasping the possibility that troops could murder a large number of Vietnamese civilians.

Another psychological factor that emerges from this conversation is the fact that Col. Henderson was still trying to make his presence felt as a new commander. He was not sure of himself and he wanted to get control of the situation. He wanted the men to see him and he wanted to see them. This is not unusual and, in fact, happens in some degree to all new commanders. But Col. Henderson's testimony on several occasions has reverted to the fact that he had to get hold of his brigade. The insecurity of the new job was exacerbated by the alleged non-combatant deaths at My Lai 4. There is no doubt that Col. Henderson questioned these men but it is extremely doubtful as to whether the questioning could have possibly served any useful purpose under the circumstances.

Col. Henderson stated after he had spoken to the soldiers at LZ Dottie then he went to the task force operation center and had them describe the landing and the operation, so he knew at that time on the 18th of March the order and the disposition of Charlie Company going through My Lai 4.

Discussions with Task Force Barker Staff
Maj. Calhoun, Task Force Barker S-3, stated[90] he was informed the night of 16 March 68 by LTC Barker that an investigation would be conducted by Col. Henderson relative to what transpired at My Lai 4. As far as he knew the investigation was being conducted to determine the facts and circumstances surrounding the killing of the one civilian as reported by the helicopter pilot, and the twenty to thirty civilians reported by Medina as being killed by artillery fire. It was not until the My Lai 4 incident appeared in the news that he was aware of any people being killed other than the

enemy reported killed on this operation. At no time was he ever aware of being questioned concerning the My Lai 4 operation by Col. Henderson.

Capt. Kotouc, the S-2[19], Capt. Lewellen, the Assistant S-3[58], and Capt. Vasquez,[18] the Artillery Liaison Officer, all stated while in Vietnam no one ever questioned them about the operation.

Col. Henderson may have gone to the Task Force Barker TOC on the afternoon of the 18th of March to determine the disposition of Charlie Company going through My Lai. However, he did not announce he was investigating anything.

Discussions with 11th Brigade Staff
Col. Henderson believed at his staff meeting the night of the 18th he would have mentioned the investigation collectively to the staff or to individually selected staff officers. He was not certain to whom he would have spoken to except that he had a recollection of having spoken to Capt. Keshel, the S-5, and perhaps at this time he also spoke to CSM Walsh.[17] He is certain selected individuals of his staff knew, his S-2 and S-3, and certainly LTC Luper. "Definitely those three individuals would have known, but I did have a reason for not publicizing it, and this was the morale of the troops. Until I had something, or something was uncovered that would lead me to believe that something did occur, I did not want a wild rumor getting spread through the brigade. I believe I cautioned Col. Barker and Maj. Calhoun and others there from Task Force Barker that I wanted this close to the belt until this had been proved or disproved." [53]

LTC Luper was not aware that Col. Henderson was conducting an investigation into the My Lai 4 operation, although Col. Henderson might have asked him on 18 March to check into the cause of twenty non-combatant casualties.

LTC Blackledge the S-2[88] was not asked by Col. Henderson for any inputs he had about the operation for inclusion in a report of investigation.

Maj. McKnight the S-3[54] knew there was an investigation conducted by Col. Henderson, but was not exactly sure how it came about, whether it was a requirement from division because of the twenty-five casualties that we had reported, or some other reason. He read the report Col. Henderson forwarded to division which was in letter form, with an explanation of the operation and the sequence of events and the scheme of the maneuver, the fire support plan and what actually happened during the conduct of the operation, and what the results were, and an explanation of how the civilian casualties occurred.

Capt. Keshel, Brigade S-5 did not receive reports from the Brigade TOC (Col. Henderson) or from Task Force Barker concerning civilian casualties as result of the 16 March operation. Therefore, he did not pay solatium or process claims as result of this operation. [83]

Capt. Pittman, 11th Brigade Provost Marshal, stated[93] that at no time when he was in Vietnam did he ever have the slightest suspicion that the personnel of Task Force Barker may have committed any unlawful acts during or after the combat assault of My Lai 4 on March 16th.

CSM Walsh had no recollection[94] of being asked by Col. Henderson to conduct an inquiry or ask questions about the operation. He was not asked by Col. Henderson to check with the people in the C/1-20th about the operation. He had no idea that there was an investigation concerning the operation. Col. Henderson in a 1970 letter asked CSM Walsh if he could recall being asked to make an inquiry among the NCO's from 1-20th Rear Area and probably C/1-20th to determine if there were any discussions or rumors concerning the My Lai incident. CSM Walsh had no recollection of being directed to question NCO's from the 1-20th Rear Area concerning My Lai operation.

MSG Russell Gross remembered[95] a few days after Col. Henderson took over the command of the 11th Infantry Brigade, that he came to our tent about 1800 hours and talked with Walsh. Henderson instructed Walsh to go over to rear area of the 1st Battalion, 20th Infantry, and talk to some of the noncommissioned officers to learn if there was any discussion going on about the operations of Task Force Barker, which he knew to be in the "Pinkville" area at that time … He did not see Walsh leave on his mission the next day, but knows he made the trip because he talked with the jeep driver, who said that he had driven Walsh to the rear area of the 1st Battalion, 20th Infantry Brigade. He never asked Walsh about what he learned while on his mission, and Walsh never discussed it with him.

It is important to note the situation with CSM Walsh. Col. Henderson recalls asking him to perform a mission and CSM Walsh, both in writing and orally denied any knowledge. Col. Henderson's recollection is substantiated by the comments of MSG Gross who remembers Col. Henderson personally talking with CSM Walsh and instructing CSM Walsh to go to rear area of 1st Battalion, 20th Infantry. Such discrepancies in recollection occurred often.

Notwithstanding Col. Henderson's probable instructions to LTC Luper and CSM Walsh it appears that Col. Henderson did not involve his staff in discussions concerning the My Lai 4 operation or in the conduct of his investigation.

There was a striking parallelism between the actions of the task force commander, the brigade commander and the division commander in that none of these senior officers in the chain of command utilized their staff or other personnel to assist in the investigation of the My Lai 4 incident. LTC Barker, effecting a cover-up, prepared his Combat After Action Report himself. Col. Henderson conducted his investigation on his own and wrote his reports of investigation on his own. MG Koster did not utilize the very large and expert division staff to assist in determining what had transpired at My Lai 4. It appears that the allegations concerning the 16 March operation of Task Force Barker were so serious that Koster and Henderson decided to keep a close hold on the information until they could determine in their mind the facts. This naturally limited their ability to investigate properly.

Discussions with Members of the 174th Aviation Company
It is possible following one of his evening staff meetings that Henderson informed Maj. Gibson, CO 174th Aviation Company, of Thompson's allegations and asked either him or two of his warrant officers to check with the pilots who supported Task Force Barker on the 16th of March and to determine if any of them had seen troops shooting wildly. He recalls not getting from either source a response as early as he needed and he either telephoned or drove up to Maj. Gibson's area and saw him and got the response from him that Gibson surveyed his pilots flying in support of Task Force Barker that day and none of his pilots observed anything out of the ordinary and that they did not observe any of his ground troops firing wildly. [17] Col. Henderson recalled he spoke to the two warrant officers after the 21st of March, the day he was wounded.

Maj. Gibson[91] had personal contact with Col. Henderson three or four times a week. From 16 to 20 March 1968, he did not think anything unusual was happening. He had no reports of gunships being out of control and he did not conduct an investigation about this operation nor did he assist anyone in an investigation about this operation.

It is concluded that Col. Henderson probably did not request Maj. Gibson or his warrant officers to survey the pilots of 174th Aviation Company and if he had Col. Henderson's oral report to MG Koster on 20 March was incorrect with regards to the pilots surveyed since he did not receive a response until after the 21st of March.

Review of Col. Henderson's Actions
Colonel Henderson indicates that immediately following BG Young's directive to investigate WO Thompson's allegations of the indiscriminate killing of civilians Col. Henderson interviewed in order: the pilots, LTC Barker and Capt. Medina. These were the only probative actions he took. The aviators (one, two or three) definitely described about 100 non-combatant casualties, including a large number bunched together in a ditch. On the other hand, both Barker and Medina falsely assured Henderson that Charlie Company was engaged with the enemy and there had been no indiscriminate killings of civilians. After talking with Medina, Henderson "had no feelings that anything wrong had occurred". These feelings were naively reinforced after his talk at LZ Dottie with a few troops returning from the field because "not a single man was trying to avoid my eye … and I still believe these were not soldiers who had just come out of the field after killing a bunch of women and children." That was what he wanted to believe, and Barker and Medina's lies precluded him from mentally grasping the actual situation. Henderson's mind was closed to the fact that his troops could have indiscriminately killed civilians.

In the other discussions Henderson had he did not probe into Thompson's allegations and when his actions are compared to what he could have done, he comes up short.

At the conclusion of the aforementioned actions which were primarily completed in an eight hour period on 18 March, Col. Henderson terminated his investigation and reported the results to MG Koster on 20 March. His investigative efforts were poorly planned, woefully insufficient and grossly inadequate. He did nothing to ascertain the causes of non-combatant casualties.

Actions Col. Henderson Might have Taken
Up to this point those actions Col. Henderson has claimed he accomplished in preparing his oral report of investigation for MG Koster have been reviewed. Therefore, the analysis to date has been on the positive aspects of what was accomplished. However, a complete impartial review of Col. Henderson's conduct of the investigation must include all actions which a prudent investigating officer might be expected to accomplish.

The major actions which Col. Henderson might have been expected to perform and which he did not accomplish are listed as follows:

(1) He didn't make any effort to talk individually to platoon leaders and key noncommissioned officers.

(2) He didn't ask WO Thompson or anyone else to describe the location of non-combatant casualties.

(3) He didn't request an individual breakdown as to how people were injured or wounded.

(4) He didn't request the Aero Scouts to reconnoiter My Lai 4 on either the afternoon of the 16th or the 17th of March after his order to resweep had been countermanded.

(5) He didn't request information through Vietnamese channels as to what had occurred at My Lai 4 on 16 March.

(6) He didn't discuss with Capt. Medina or Lt. Calley the pilot's confrontation.

(7) He didn't ask to plot the location of artillery rounds on the map.

(8) He didn't reconcile non-combatant casualties with the impact area of artillery or gunships.

(9) He didn't determine whether gunships had fired in support of Charlie Company troops.

(10) He didn't ask Capt. Medina if he or his troops had gone down the North-South trail where Col. Henderson had observed non-combatant bodies.

(11) He didn't discuss cross-fires.

(12) He didn't discuss tactics and employment with Capt. Medina.

(13) He didn't receive a breakdown of total VC and non-combatant casualties by company.

(14) He didn't discuss the sixty-nine VC KIA's caused by artillery.

(15) He didn't review the logs of Task Force Barker or 11th Brigade.

(16) He didn't discuss how many VC from the 48th Battalion had been sighted and how many had escaped and evaded.

(17) He didn't determine whether artillery had fired in support of Charlie Company troops.

It is doubtful if a seasoned brigade commander could have taken most or all of the aforementioned actions which Col. Henderson failed to accomplish. This was his first day in the field as brigade commander and his first combat assault. Col. Henderson also had three additional battalions to supervise, several of which were in contact with the enemy. A quick commander's inquiry could not possibly have touched all those bases. It is difficult to comprehend all of the demands of a brigade commander's time during daily combat and it is easy several years later to list possible actions a prudent investigating officer might accomplish in isolation from his other duties.

Col. Henderson relied very heavily on LTC Barker's and Capt. Medina's inputs concerning the conduct of the battle and they were giving him false observations. There is no doubt that Col. Henderson could have delved much more deeply into the actions of Task Force Barker on 16 March 1971. For example, if he had taken the simple step of ordering an over flight of My Lai 4 or even had talked to Mr. Millians who flew on the 16th and overflew My Lai 4 on the 17th observing very many dead women and children, the alleged atrocities probably would have been verified.

It is important to note that as a brigade commander in a combat zone with four infantry battalions operating in a split area of operations Col. Henderson had his hands full. For example, on 16 March he observed the operations of Task Force Barker, met with MG Koster, visited MG Toan the CG of the 2nd ARVN Division and the ranking Vietnamese officer in the region, attended to duties at his headquarters and that afternoon visited the operations of the 4th/3rd Infantry Battalion west of Highway 1 that was in contact with the enemy and calling for tactical air strikes. Nevertheless, he had adequate time prior to 20 March to conduct a much more thorough investigation.

When those actions which Col. Henderson took are compared to those actions which he might have accomplished one could reasonably presume that Col. Henderson either willfully failed to thoroughly and properly investigate or that he was grossly negligent in the conduct of his investigation.

THE REPORTS OF INVESTIGATION

Col. Henderson discussed his 20 March oral report to MG Koster as follows:[17] "It is my feeling, that when I talked to MG Koster, that it wasn't any five or ten minute discussion, it was twenty to thirty minutes and I was doing most of the talking. So I am certain that I went into greater detail as to exactly who I talked to when. And it was all related to the helicopter pilot, but the exact finding that I had not found or uncovered anything to substantiate the warrant officer pilot's allegations, except the fact that he had seen a captain shoot a woman and this has been attested to by Capt. Medina."[53]

"I felt that basically I wound up that the—based on this inquiry of mine that the allegations of wild and indiscriminate shooting by my ground troops was not substantiated. I explained to him the circumstances of the captain shooting the woman. I explained to him the marking of additional wounded personnel by smoke, by the warrant officer pilot. "

Col. Henderson advised MG Koster that WO Thompson was the only one who saw something unusual and he was confused about what he had seen. Although there was some truth to his allegations, they were exaggerated. He was excitable and emotional and his report could not be substantiated.

He also discussed the report he received from LTC Barker concerning the twenty non-combatant casualties which had been written down on a 3x5 card. There was a breakout by men, women and children and how they had been killed, reflecting that they had been killed equally by either gunships or artillery fire.

MG Koster[68] in discussing his meeting with Col. Henderson stated: "I learned that Henderson interrogated a great many people from the rifle company that had been on the ground, talked to the company commanders. I am sure his words to me at one time were, he had talked to all the aviators who had been over the area. But I questioned whether he really talked to all of them, but certainly had the feeling that he talked to representative aviators who had been over the area."

"I was assured by Henderson that as he went along in this inquiry, and

130

many times the information was brought to me by BG Young … and I suspect that some of it might have come directly from LTC Barker, that the troops had conducted themselves properly, that this was a contested combat action and that the casualties had been incurred during the course of this contested action…"

"I know that Col. Henderson said that he came up and what he thought was the wrap up and gave it to me in my office in Chu Lai. I don't remember having any formal version saying here's my investigation all laid out. It was more apt to—it was more likely to be, you know I talked to company commanders I told you about that, I talked to the men in the company, platoon leaders and sergeants. I talked to aviators and this is what I concluded… He had a great deal of additional information. He had all the information he had obtained from all the people he had interrogated." [68]

When Col. Henderson was told MG Koster believed that he had talked to substantially all of the aviators, and a large number of people in Charlie Company that had been on the ground that day, he replied, "I certainly did not give him this impression I'm positive."

Col. Henderson had at best only superficial knowledge of what had transpired, and was relying primarily on inputs from LTC Barker and Capt. Medina. His report was based on a shallow and incomplete investigation and gave a false impression of the circumstances. Regardless of its brevity, Col. Henderson's oral report was accepted. That is not surprising since both MG Koster and he were obtaining almost all of their information from the same source – LTC Barker.

Col. Henderson alleges that in addition to his oral report to MG Koster on 20 March he submitted two other reports and endorsed a formal report prepared by LTC Barker, all concerning the Task Force Barker operation on 16 March. LTC Barker also submitted a Combat Action Report on the activities of Task Force Barker during 16-19 March in response to a request from division headquarters for a report on the activities of C Company 1/20 Infantry on 16 March. A document-collection team methodically went through the files of all the organizations associated with My Lai 4 assiduously searching for any document pertaining to the incident. Col. Henderson's Report of Investigation submitted in late March or early April and LTC Barkers' Report of Investigation submitted about mid-May, which was endorsed by Col. Henderson, could not be found. However, Col. Henderson provided his 24 April report which he had in his possession. It is important to determine as much as possible the substance of the reports of investigations.

Col. Henderson remembers[17] about ten days to two weeks after he had given his oral report to MG Koster that BG Young advised him MG Koster wanted his oral report in writing. He recalled very vividly asking BG Young if there had been some new development or was there something he did not know about? BG Young replied, there's nothing new but MG Koster wants the report for the record. At that time Col. Henderson wrote a three to five page document on the investigation that he had conducted concerning the incident and hand carried it to the Americal Division. This was before he had obtained the VC propaganda message.

Major McKnight, 11th Brigade S-3, supported Col. Henderson's claim that he submitted his oral report in writing to MG Koster in the latter part of March or first of April.[54] He recalled that Col. Henderson prepared two reports, the second was initiated because of some VC propaganda. Maj. McKnight assumed Col. Henderson was directed by MG Koster to conduct an investigation. He read the report Col. Henderson forwarded to division. It was in letter form, with an explanation of the operation and the sequence of events and the scheme of the maneuver, the fire support plan and what actually happened during the conduct of the operation, and what the results were, and an explanation of how the civilian casualties occurred. The subject was reopened at a later time in April, because the S-2, LTC Blackledge, had received through ARVN channels a propaganda leaflet which stated we had massacred or slaughtered something like 300 to 400 people. Col. Henderson as a matter of course brought this to the division commander's attention. He also discussed it with the 2nd ARVN Division commander and Maj. McKnight was present during that discussion.

Although Col. Henderson's written report concerning the helicopter pilot's allegations has never been found it is believed that it existed. Since it conveyed no new information to MG Koster, its loss is not considered of great importance.

Col. Henderson states the next thing he heard about the incident was a letter which came from the Quang Ngai Province headquarters and a VC propaganda message which was delivered to his S-2, LTC Blackledge, about the middle of April. It is believed that letter was obtained through the liaison officer from the 52nd Military Intelligence Detachment which reported to LTC Trexler the G-2. Col. Henderson sent a copy of the propaganda leaflet to Americal Division headquarters through intelligence channels. This was about 14 April.

Several days later Young came down to Duc Pho and said the VC propaganda message Col. Henderson sent up has tripped MG Koster's memory and he wants some backup in the files here should anything further develop on the matter and to provide him with a written report. As a result of this Col. Henderson wrote a report from his notes which he had taken down when Thompson had related the incident to him and forwarded the report to division on or about the 24th of April. He did not make any additional investigating efforts.

About the 10th of May BG Young instructed Col. Henderson that MG Koster desired a formal investigation of this incident be conducted. BG Young had no knowledge of any additional data which the division commander might have. Col. Henderson told BG Young if he had no objections, he would assign LTC Barker, who was now his executive officer, to conduct the investigation. BG Young indicated this was satisfactory. When asked[17] if it didn't seem unusual to have somebody investigating himself, Col. Henderson replied at no point at this time had he been led to believe or had any information that Col. Barker was personally involved in this. It never entered his mind that Barker was investigating something which took place in units under his command.

Col. Henderson received no directives in writing from the division and he gave verbal instructions to Col. Barker telling him that MG Koster wanted a formal investigation and he was to take statements from anybody and everybody who was directly or indirectly related to this incident and that he wanted these statements taken in adequate detail to prove or disprove that anything had taken place. Col. Henderson issued instructions to LTC Barker the same day that BG Young gave them to him which was around the 10th of May.

Specialist Michael DiFilippo Jr. who was assigned to the 11th Brigade personnel section stated[97] he typed an endorsement to correspondence that had to do with Task Force Barker. He said there were hand-written statements with what he was typing. He recalls typing from a hand-written statement which he thought was a draft in Col. Henderson's handwriting. He had typed from Col. Henderson's handwriting before, and he was familiar with his handwriting. The file contained a basic letter about three or four pages long, some other typed material, and some hand-written statements on some forms similar to witness statement forms. He stated that the file was about 3/4 of an inch thick. The length of the endorsement was about one and one-half pages. It was classified CONFIDENTIAL.

Col. Henderson's recollection concerning LTC Barker's formal investigation, which is also recalled by MG Koster, is bolstered by the testimony of LTC Barney Brannen Jr., the Americal Division Staff Judge Advocate, who saw such a report in May 1969.[98] The over-all file which Brannen saw was about one half inch thick. There were at least six statements, and perhaps as many as thirty, but he could not remember how many pages there were. The statement by the investigating officer was signed, but he cannot remember if it was signed by LTC Barker or not. He stated that he knows that it was not a full colonel. The statement was similar to the following: this is an investigation about alleged civilian casualties and deaths during the operation of Task Force Barker at My Lai in mid-March 1968. It went on to describe the area of operations, it described the way the operation started, the number of units involved and what units. It mentioned the preparatory fires and that the civilian deaths were the result of those fires. The body of the witness statements were written in the same hand and signed by different people.

It is concluded there appeared to be five reports: Col. Henderson's oral report (20 March); Col. Henderson's oral report reduced to writing (27 March to 10 April) which has not been found; Col. Henderson's letter of transmittal forwarding the VC propaganda leaflet with background information (24 April); LTC Barker's formal investigation endorsed by Col. Henderson (mid-May) which included signed statements by participants in the operation which has not been found; and LTC Barker's Combat Action Report of 28 March.

MG Koster on four occasions directed that investigations be made of the incidents reported by WO Thompson at My Lai 4 on 16 March. In each instance the order was transmitted by BG Young to Col. Henderson. In three cases, with the exception of the written report of Col. Henderson's oral report, the reports of investigations were acknowledged by MG Koster. He has stated the reports were satisfactory.

The question remains were Thompson's allegations properly investigated? With respect to Col. Henderson's oral report, when the actions he undertook are compared to those he might have been expected to perform, it appears that Col. Henderson was definitely negligent in the performance of his investigation. He made no further investigative attempts to support his written report of early April or for his 24 April report. Henderson had observed little of the operation and was totally dependent upon the field reporting of LTC Barker and Capt. Medina, both of whom assured him as part of their cover-up that there was an engagement with the enemy and the troops had conducted themselves properly. He accepted their inputs and failed to aggressively follow-up on Thompson's allegations.

LTC Barker's combat action report of 28 March again gave the false impression of a contested battle. He wrote that the initial artillery preparation resulted in sixty-eight VC KIA's in the enemy outpost positions and then Charlie Company immediately attacked to the east receiving enemy small arms fire as they proceeded forward. However, there was no enemy; no enemy fire; and sixty-eight VC killed by artillery was false. Barker's combat action report was a sham. Likewise his formal report of mid-May which included from ten to thirty signed attachments from the participants in the operation. Not one of the many personnel interviewed by the Peer's Inquiry stated they signed a statement. Barker's reports purposely extended the myth of a contested battle at My Lai 4.

MG Koster recalls that the signed statements in the Barker investigation were submitted by "company commanders, platoon leaders, aviators and artillerymen." It is presumed that Koster and Henderson read at least some of the signed statements. Yet, neither took the effort to discuss a forged statement with its falsely identified originator. If they had, it would have exposed Barker's elaborate cover-up of the assault.

Review of the Investigations
Division aviators and Vietnamese as well reported hundreds of dead non-combatants resulting from the assault whereas Task Force Barker reported 128 VC killed and only 20 non-combatant casualties. Efforts by the headquarters to resolve this reporting dichotomy reads like a melodrama – the good guys (aviators) versus the bad guys (those covering-up).

The occurrence of non-combatant casualties (but not the full extent of the killing) at My Lai 4 was reported expeditiously to MG Koster and by noon the next day he was briefed on WO Thompsons' observances. He immediately ordered an investigation which was carried out by Col. Henderson.

On the 18th Henderson was directed at LZ Dottie to investigate WO Thompson's allegations. His first action was to immediately interview Thompson, the pilot who was young and on his first combat assault. During the interview Thompson was nervous and emotional. He said he had definitely seen over a hundred civilian casualties but admitted he had seen only one person shot. Henderson doubted Thompson and rationalized what the pilot observed that morning were the 128 VC and perhaps some of the 20 non-combatants.

Right after interviewing Thompson, Henderson met with Barker at LZ
Dottie and then with Medina at his field position. Consider that 16 March
was Henderson's second day in command and it was his first combat
assault. That morning he managed to fritter away his overview of the
assault and had not seen any of Charlie Company's actions. He was totally
dependent upon Barker's and Medina's inputs about the assault.
Henderson was unsure of himself and was facing a fouled-up situation with
the civilian casualties. Both Barker and Medina were strong leaders telling
the same story and both were adamant that there was a battle and there was
no indiscriminant shooting. Henderson, in no position to disagree,
accepted their version of events. He never considered more than twenty
civilian casualties – his mind was closed to considering a major atrocity.

Gen. Koster was briefed by Barker at LZ Dottie on both the 16th and 18th
and orally by Henderson on the 20th. Both assured him that there was a
battle and no indiscriminate shooting, and provided him a wrap-up of 128
VC body count and 20 non-combatant casualties. Henderson was
subsequently directed to submit his oral report in writing. Koster, relying
on his commanders, also accepted their story. Thus the chain of command
was focused not on the hundreds of non-combatants killed but only upon
20 civilian casualties that should have been duly reported.

Later when a VC leaflet mentioning that "500 people who had empty
hands" had been killed, was obtained by Col. Henderson and forwarded to
division headquarters it tripped MG Koster's memory and he requested a
written report about the assault from Henderson who forwarded it on 24
April. Afterwards, about 10 May, MG Koster desiring additional backup
information ordered a thorough formal investigation of the matter, which
was performed by LTC Barker and endorsed by Henderson. Barker again
falsely reiterated that there had been a contested conflict and over twenty
civilians had been unfortunately killed. Koster and Henderson who had
kept the matter of non-combatant deaths to themselves and had not
involved their respective staffs in the investigations both immediately but
separately went to the Vietnamese authorities to discuss the contents of the
VC leaflet. The Vietnamese assured them that it was VC propaganda.

The Division Headquarters early on the 16th promptly retransmitted LTC
Barker's spot report of 128 VC body count to Headquarters MACV and
shortly thereafter the MACV Commander sent a message congratulating
the officers and men of Charlie Company for their outstanding actions.
The MACV congratulatory message befuddled the men of Charlie
Company but it was well received by Barker and Medina, the cover-up co-
conspirators, who were aggressively telling MG Koster and Col.

Henderson, their senior commanders, a concocted story that The Task Force Barker Assault was a contested battle where 128 VC and 20 non-combatants were killed. Unfortunately, both Koster and Henderson bought into Barker's false story. Since all five of the investigative reports submitted to the division headquarters were authored by either Henderson or Barker, the real results of Charlie Company's assault never came to light.

The Americal Division investigations were inadequate and misleading, providing the impression of a contested enemy fire-fight which resulted in 128 VC killed in hostile action. They failed to uncover the atrocities which had occurred.

Follow-up actions by division headquarters personnel regarding My Lai 4 were totally ineffective. WO Thompson, somewhat disgruntled, frequently requested the status of the investigation into the non-combatant casualties and his concerns were often brought to the attention of Col. Parsons by LTC Lewis. The chief of staff who was informed almost immediately did not grasp the situation and failed to utilize his special staff to assist Henderson in his investigation. He recalled little, although an enlisted man in his office clearly remembered him having multiple conversations in May with US provincial advisors concerning the VC propaganda leaflet. The G-2, G-3 and G-5 all were informed of non-combatant casualties, yet they remembered nothing and did nothing. The senior aviation officers, LTC Holliday and Maj. Watke, after WO Thompson's initial report, never again questioned their pilots. In mid-May when Barker submitted his investigation supported by ten or more signed false statements neither Koster or Henderson questioned a participant, which would have determined they had not signed a statement. There were many loose ends to Barker's story which if examined could debunk it, but division headquarters failed to pursue any of these.

Assured by Henderson, Barker, Medina and the Vietnamese, Koster let the matter of My Lai 4 rest, unaware that Barker, Medina and the soldiers of Charlie Company, including the public information personnel, were involved in a very effective cover-up of the atrocities at My Lai 4.

When General Westmoreland visited the 11th Brigade on 20 April 1968 MG Koster had the opportunity to inform him of the non-combatant casualties and the content of the VC propaganda leaflet, and he did not. Consequently, no civilian casualties, much less the full extent of the atrocities, were ever reported to higher headquarters by the Americal Division. The Americal Division headquarters had failed to successfully resolve the initial reporting dichotomy – Were those killed at My Lai 4 non-combatants or Viet Cong?. The "bad guys" had won – the cover-up was successful.

General Westmoreland's Visit to the 11th Brigade
In December 1969 an important bit of information was unearthed, that is, Item 74 in the 11th Brigade log on 20 April, one month after My Lai 4, which indicated Gen. Westmoreland, the MACV commander, visited 11th Brigade headquarters at Duc Pho. This fact was surprising because the visit had not been revealed previously either by the extensive Peers Inquiry or the Koster Article 32 investigation.

Mr. Richard Blackledge,[88] who formerly as a LTC was the 11th Brigade intelligence officer, attended the briefing. On 3 Dec 1970 he recalled that Gen. Westmoreland was briefed on three 11th Brigade operations: My Lai 4; Operation Norfolk Victory; and when an enemy ship coming from North Vietnam was forced to beach and was blown up by its crew. The My Lai 4 operation was briefed as a success and the 128 body count was mentioned. LTC Blackledge could not recall if there was mention of twenty non-combatant casualties or if the Viet Cong propaganda leaflet describing 500 men, women, and children being killed. It is obvious that neither subject was mentioned because Gen. Westmoreland has been quoted as saying that he was aware of the operation of Task Force Barker and remembered it had been quite successful -- 128 Viet Cong had been killed – but there had been no indications that civilians had been involved in anyway, much less that atrocities or war crimes had been committed.[88]

It is important to note that the two key officers in the chain of command concerning the My Lai 4 incident were both on hand at Gen. Westmoreland's briefing. MG Koster who had directed investigations to be made and then reviewed the investigative reports and Col. Henderson who conducted the investigations into WO Thompson's allegations. Both officers knew within two hours of the initial combat assault that six to eight non-combatants had been killed and both knew late in the day that twenty to twenty-eight non-combatants had been killed. Both were aware prior to the 20 April briefing that the My Lai 4 village chief had complained American troops killed 450 villagers and there was a Viet Cong document circulated that mentioned "… the Americans … killed 500 people who had empty hands in the Tinh Khe (Song My Village)…" Yet both focused on 20 non-combatant casualties and were never aware of the magnitude of the massacre

These two officers by their actions and their words were greatly concerned in preventing civilian non-combatant casualties. Neither one had checked their unit logs to see if non-combatant casualties had been reported, which considering all of their required duties at the time was certainly understandable. However, without their logs reflecting civilian casualties there was no way higher headquarters could have been informed, which they were not. Now, on 20 April was the opportunity to inform the commander-in-chief of the Vietnamese civilian casualties which occurred and to mention the VC propaganda leaflet.

It was MG Koster's responsibility in the chain of command to report the civilian casualties and the contents of the VC leaflet to his next higher headquarters. Given this opportunity to inform the MACV commander, he did not. His failure to do so was certainly an egregious omission of his responsibility to inform his superiors of the non-combatant incidents of My Lai 4.

Suppose that MG Koster had informed Gen. Westmoreland, what could have been the outcome? Most probably Gen. Westmoreland would have said "Please investigate the situation further and keep me informed." Subsequently MG Koster did direct a thorough formal investigation. Unbelievably, the investigation was conducted by LTC Barker, the complicit Task Force commander. Why BG Young and MG Koster allowed that to happen without a collateral investigation by the division staff is baffling. LTC Barker's patently false investigation was recalled as having numerous sworn statements by operational participants. Yet, none of the large number of key personnel investigated by the Peers Inquiry ever remember signing a statement. MG Koster was purposely misled and obviously Gen. Westmoreland would never have been informed.

On the other hand, since the impetus for a further investigation would have come from Gen. Westmoreland, perhaps MG Koster would have utilized his special staff and personally paid more attention to the investigation so that the false reporting could have been discovered and perhaps the full extent of the civilian atrocities at My Lai 4 would have come to light in Vietnam.

THE TASK FORCE BARKER COVER-UP

Once LTC Barker realized the large number of civilian casualties, he initiated a cover-up which was abetted by Capt. Medina and the soldiers of Charlie Company, including the public information personnel.

The concept of Barker's orchestrated cover-up was simple and effective. First, he and Medina had to convince the chain of command, i.e. Koster and Henderson, that it was a contested assault and non-combatants were not indiscriminately killed. Then they had to ensure that all reports conveyed the same message: Henderson's; the PIO newspaper article; the After Action Report; and Barker's in-depth investigation. Finally, and most important, they had to take steps to see that the assault participants did not discuss the incident, even amongst themselves.

The cover-up was initiated almost immediately. An hour after its combat assault Charlie Company reported eighty-four enemy killed. LTC Barker after waiting a period of fifty minutes decided to report sixty-nine of the body count as VC killed by artillery in a location a good distance from My Lai 4 and far from the location reported by Charlie Company, although there was no mention of artillery in the Charlie Company message. The subterfuge was to make the civilian casualties appear as VC killed by artillery and gunships and not by small arms fire.

On the afternoon of the assault Barker provided false information in a debrief of the PIO personnel which was written up and published. Both PIO personnel were complicit in the cover-up. They had clearly observed the killing of women and children and the burning of the hamlet. Haeberle took vivid color photographs of the mayhem which he kept for himself, turning in bland black and white photos which portrayed no violations. Roberts wrote an article citing 128 enemy killed in a battle which was published in the division newspaper and later in the Stars and Stripes keeping alive the fiction that My Lai 4 was a victory over the VC.

Later on the 18th Barker told Medina to advise his troops not to discuss the assault among themselves or with anybody else. Medina called his company together to do just that and also to inform them that an investigation was being conducted. Medina was a strong leader respected by his troops and it is doubtful if a lesser commander could have kept the lid on something as serious as the killing of hundreds of women and children. The deception continued.

Barker forcefully informed Koster and Henderson on the 18th that it was a contested action and he assured them that the troops had conducted themselves properly. Medina told Henderson that civilians had been killed by artillery and gunships and denied there had been indiscriminate shooting. These assurances were accepted by Koster and Henderson notwithstanding Thompson's allegations.

On the 16th and the 18th both Barker and Medina vociferously rejected Henderson' directives to return to My Lai for the purpose of determining casualties.

LTC Barker managed to obtain and to respond to the Division's directive addressed to the 11th Brigade to provide an After Action Report of Charlie Company's activities on March 16. His blatantly false report did not focus on Charlie Company, but covered Task Force Barker's actions between 16-19 March. This was another step in covering-up the extent of non-combatant casualties. LTC Barker in both his After Action Report and his formal investigation wrote that the assault was a contested conflict, when in fact there was no enemy opposition. Additionally his formal Report of Investigation falsely enclosed from ten to thirty forged individual accounts to cover-up the real situation.

The participant's cover-up succeeded because of the incompetence of those receiving the reports and investigating the incident. Barker's instantaneous reactions to his knowledge of the extensive non-combatant killings and his on-the-run efforts to cover-up the scope of the atrocities were amazing. The cover-up's success boggles the mind, since there were so many opportunities to debunk the participants false reporting.

For example:

- If Koster had probed Henderson's oral report.
- If Henderson had insisted on viewing the casualties.
- If LTC Luper had made an artillery investigation, as required.
- If the Province Chief had investigated the incident, as directed.

- If Koster or Henderson had questioned any of those who allegedly signed statements.
- If Parsons had used his special staff to assist in the investigation of the incident.
- If Koster had informed General Westmoreland of the non-combatant casualties
- If only <u>one</u> infantryman had spoken out, orally or in writing.

Contrary to prevalent opinions, there was no collusion at every level of command to conceal the My Lai 4 incident. The My Lai 4 cover-up was effected by the two combat assault leaders, LTC Barker and Capt. Medina. Medina under oath admitted participating in the cover-up, claiming his motivations were to avoid disgracing the Army and concerns for himself and his family.

Most regrettably LTC Barker, the tough, proud combat soldier, along with Capt. Michles was killed while on an operation on 13 June 1968, thus investigators were obviously unable to obtain Barker's inputs concerning the operation. One can only imagine that LTC Barker was aghast when he determined the scope of Charlie Company's actions, and believing his orders were grossly misconstrued, he determined to conceal what actually occurred.

The Barker and Medina led cover-up to divert attention from the mass slaughter was so successful that knowledge of the true extent of the killings at My Lai 4 was kept unknown for over a year and was never discovered in Vietnam.

A REVIEW OF COL. HENDERSON'S CHARGES

In late January 1970 most of the charges against the other individuals subject to Article 32 investigations had been dismissed. Only Col. Henderson's and 1st Lt. Dennis Johnson's Article 32s were on-going. To date no one had been held accountable for the military offenses of failing to make official reports or who had failed to order or had not followed up investigations with references to the killing of non-combatants at My Lai 4 on 16 March 1968. Evidence supports the fact that Col. Henderson failed to conduct a thorough investigation and the vital question is: was he negligent or willful in his failure to adequately perform his duties.

Many senior officers who had served with Col. Henderson for several years in various capacities held him in high esteem with important qualities of dedication, self-sacrifice, intelligence and courage of his convictions. They all had a great deal of trust and confidence in his character and integrity, stating that he always accepted responsibility and would not shift the blame. These senior officers of mature judgment and valued service to the United States Army described Col. Henderson as a dedicated, sincere, intelligent and truthful officer upon whom they had a great amount of trust and confidence. On the other hand, government counsel believed that Col. Henderson lied each time he has testified, and that he has intentionally lied while under oath.

In December 1970 government counsels submitted a brief to assist the defense. The brief was well done and noted that Col. Henderson's statements depicted an inept, bumbling attempt at conducting an investigation. His complete lack of competency or intelligence is belied by the strong character witnesses who have indicated an outstanding officer that was complete, thorough, intelligent and highly competent in every endeavor. They site as one example of several "Nowhere does it appear that Colonel Henderson made any attempt to ascertain the exact cause of the confirmed 20 civilian casualties". From the example cited it became "loud and clear" that Colonel Henderson did nothing towards conducting an investigation that was designed to produce constructive information about the allegations made by the pilot. "From all the sources of available information, he checked none, believed none of the abundant confirming facts and reports and falsely reported to Major General Koster that he had satisfied himself that there was no evidence to support the allegations." Considering the aforementioned circumstantial evidence they claim that Colonel Henderson deliberately, knowingly and intentionally avoided any attempt at an honest effort to ascertain the facts. In conclusion they state the evidence is sufficient in law and fact to support each specification as charged. If found guilty of just one specification the maximum punishment which could be imposed by a general court-martial is dismissal from the service, confinement at hard labor and a total forfeiture of payment allowances. They strongly believed that Colonel Henderson was willfully negligent in the conduct of his investigations.

An area of concern was: Did Col. Henderson know that a large number of non-combatant deaths had been alleged? This is an important point that needs resolution, because it is the key as to whether Col. Henderson acted willfully or negligently in the conduct of his investigation. Col. Henderson stated that "at no time can I recollect ever having the impression that there were a greater number than this twenty civilians."[17] Even though Col. Henderson received an allegation of at least a hundred or more non-combatants killed, he rationalized that part of the large number of non-combatants reported killed must have been the VC body count reported by Capt. Medina and in his mind the number of non-combatant casualties remained at twenty. He was adamant he never considered more than twenty non-combatant casualties.

Unlike many others who testified, Col. Henderson was always responsive and straight-forward, responding even when the answer could be considered not in his best interest. When asked if he agreed if there were an allegation of sixty to one hundred civilians killed that a commander's inquiry was hopelessly inadequate, he responded, "Absolutely."[17]

Those who reported the incident to Col Henderson had seen only one Vietnamese killed, the woman on the ground, and Capt. Medina explained that killing away somewhat plausibly. He had no other firsthand reports of killing at My Lai 4. For him to have vigorously pursued an investigation over the positive statements of no wrongdoing by both subordinate commanders, LTC Barker and Capt. Medina, he would have had to picture the wanton killing of women and children. US officers are not conditioned to think of their men as ruthless killers of women and children. Col. Henderson, throughout 25 years of honorable service, had learned to respect his troops. The men in his units, mostly draftees, represented the cross-section of American youth. Col. Henderson in his letter to General Westmoreland stated: "I continue to maintain the highest admiration, confidence, and faith in the integrity, fighting qualities and courage of the officers and men, 11th LIB, present during the alleged incident." [99]

Although Col. Henderson was apprised of the large number of non-combatants killed he continued to maintain in his mind the impression that there were twenty and that he did not willfully fail to conduct a proper investigation nor did he consciously attempt to suppress information. His actions were <u>grossly inadequate</u>.

Oran K. Henderson was charged with one specification among several of dereliction of duty in that he willfully failed to conduct a thorough and proper investigation of allegations or reports of excessive killing of non-combatants, and a confrontation between a helicopter pilot and ground forces; and one specification of failing to obey a lawful general regulation, MACV Directive 20-4, dated 27 April 1967, in that he did not report to his commanding officer incidents and acts thought or alleged to be war crimes, the intentional infliction of death or injury upon non-combatant Vietnamese civilians, both in violation of Article 92, Uniform Code of Military Justice.

With respect to the specification of failing to report the killing of non-combatants, testimony failed to indicate that Col. Henderson had any reports, with the exception of Capt. Medina's shooting a woman, that there was any intentional infliction of death or injury upon non-combatant Vietnamese human beings. Col. Henderson personally reported non-combatant deaths to the commanding general of the Americal Division on two occasions on 16 March 1968 and in his oral report of 20 March to Gen Koster and in his 24 March report. Col. Henderson failed to obey MACV Directive 20-4 in that he did not report the unlawful burning of houses at My Lai 4. He knew there was burning of houses yet, he failed to mention this when he made his reports to MG Koster. Still the torching of houses was not included in the specifications. This specification was not supported by the evidence submitted.

With respect to the specification of willfully failing to conduct a thorough and proper investigation; had Col. Henderson willfully failed to conduct a proper and thorough investigation this was a severe offense and a general court-martial certainly would be in order. However, if he acted negligently then administrative punishment would be more in line with the severity of the offense. Both the Peer's Inquiry and the Article 32 trial judge advocate, based upon circumstantial evidence believed that Col. Henderson had willfully failed to conduct a proper investigation. This would seem to make him complicit in the Task Force Barker led cover-up, yet both Barker and Medina continuously lied in their reports to Col. Henderson.

Based on the facts of the case and the personalities involved it could be surmised that no court-martial board would ever convict Col. Henderson of the charges preferred against him for the following reasons:

- Col. Henderson by his actions and words was very concerned in maintaining the safety of non-combatants
- He personally had not witnessed the killing of any Vietnamese
- His orders for Charlie Company to retrace its movements and determine the number and cause of death of non-combatants was countermanded by MG Koster.
- Both senior officers in the chain of command, BG Young and MG Koster, had their charges dismissed. However, subsequently they both were administratively censured and the Secretary of the Army vacated Koster's rank of temporary major general, reducing him to his permanent grade of brigadier general.
- He had always been straightforward, answering all questions and never shirking or evading as so many other officers had. He appeared forthright and responsible and made an excellent impression.
- Several senior officers who had served with him testified that he was held in high esteem for his important qualities of dedication, self-sacrifice and courage of convictions. He was not the type to lie to protect himself from blame and criticism. These officers had a great deal of trust and confidence in him.
- His service to the nation was exemplary. He fought as an infantryman in three wars, was wounded four times and had been awarded five Silver Stars for gallantry.
- LTC Barker and Capt. Medina lied in their discussions with him indicating he was not complicit in their cover-up.
- Both American and Vietnamese who received the VC propaganda leaflet did not believe that American troops would purposely machine gun and kill over 400 old men, women and children.
- There were many extenuating circumstances affecting his conduct of the investigation such as: the orders were not precise as to the method and what to investigate and report; there was no offer of assistance; he had three other battalions to supervise; etc.

If it was probable that a general court-martial board would not find Col. Henderson guilty, then the question of trial by general court-martial became very important. Should he be tried by general court-martial and found not guilty, then no officer would have been punished for failing to properly investigate the My Lai 4 incident. Col. Henderson was the key officer involved in investigating the alleged offenses which occurred at My Lai 4. Evidence indicated he was definitely negligent, <u>even grossly so</u>, in his investigative performance and most probably he should be punished. Non-judicial punishment under Article 15 would be <u>certain</u> and in the investigating officer's judgment would be in consonance with his failure, considering the extenuating circumstances and all the other important duties he was performing in a battle environment. Considering that the potential punishment outcomes with an Article 15 were more in line with Henderson's failure to adequately investigate WO Thompson's allegations and the opinion that Henderson would be found not guilty in a trial by general court-martial, it was recommended that the specification to the charge Violation of the Uniform Code of Military Justice, Article 92. "that he willfully failed to conduct a proper and thorough investigation, as it was his duty to do so" be amended to read negligently instead of willfully and that Col. Henderson be administered non-judicial punishment under Article 15, Uniform Code of Military Justice; and any administrative actions deemed necessary. The Report of Investigation was submitted to the convening authority on 18 February 1971.

Subsequently on 20 February 1971 The First US Army Staff Judge Advocate submitted to the convening authority his "Advice on the Disposition of the Courts-martial Charges" which included a detailed multi-page summary of the proceedings.[100] The staff judge advocate disagreed with the recommended investigative findings with respect to the charge of failing to conduct a proper or thorough investigation. He agreed that Colonel Henderson's investigation was woefully inadequate and felt that it was intentionally so, stating "… there is sufficient evidence, circumstantial and otherwise, to establish that Colonel Henderson was in fact willfully derelict.". With respect to the Charge of failing to report incidents and acts alleged to be war crimes he felt there was sufficient evidence to support the specification. The staff judge advocate recommended trial by general courts-martial.

LTG Jonathan Seaman, the First US Army Commander and convening authority, after thoroughly considering both the Report of Investigation and the Advice of the Staff Judge Advocate directed trial by general court-martial as recommended by the staff judge advocate. Not realizing that LTG Seaman had retired and been succeeded by LTG Clare E. Hutchin, the investigating officer was surprised when LTG Hutchin called from Fort Meade and requested him to review the Henderson Article 32 with him at 0900 hours on a Sunday morning. At the meeting that morning only he and MG Richard Ciccolella, LTG Hutchin's chief of staff, were present during the three hour review of the Report of Investigation. The most pertinent aspects of the investigation were highlighted and those factors which might result in an acquittal should Col. Henderson be court-martialed were discussed in detail. Non-judicial punishment under Article 15 was again recommended for two reasons: first, the punishments that could be meted out administratively were more in consonance with the offense of negligently failing to conduct a proper investigation of the pilot's allegations; second, if tried and found not guilty by a general court-martial then no one in the American Division would have been punished for failing to properly investigate the atrocities that occurred at My Lai 4. LTG Hutchin said that his staff judge advocate and the Article 32 trial judge advocate both strongly recommended trial by general court-martial. The counsels definitely believed they could prove that Henderson had willfully failed to conduct a thorough and proper investigation, inferring that he was complicit in the cover-up. They recommended that the convening authority approve a trial by general court martial where, if Henderson were to be convicted, a heavier punishment could result, even dismissal from the service. There was no doubt that Col. Henderson was definitely negligent but not willfully so. At the conclusion of the lengthy meeting LTG Hutchin said he had to further review the situation. LTG Hutchin was in a tough spot, he too realized that no officer yet had been held responsible for the fact that the atrocities had not been properly investigated and reported in South Vietnam. It would be difficult for him to overrule his staff legal officers, but hopefully he would do so.

LTG Hutchin preferred charges for general court-martial proceedings. By referring Col. Henderson's charges to court-martial the convening authority made a deliberate decision to seek a greater potential punishment for him. Although Henderson had definitely done a poor job of investigating the incident, he was believed to be not complicit in the cover-up and he was acquitted by the general court on 17 December 1971.

CONCLUSIONS

Once the My Lai 4 situation was brought to light, the Peers Inquiry expended thousands of man-hours and millions of dollars in time of war to fully and completely investigate the incident to establish the facts, seeking to determine those who may have failed to report the incident and to have properly investigated WO Thompson's allegation.

The reporting of the non-combatant casualties at My Lai 4 was good. In all, eighteen separate reporting actions reached the Americal Division headquarters and the command section and the general staff at Americal Division headquarters all were aware by 17 March that non-combatants had been killed. However, there were serious differences in the reports received. The Vietnamese, both friendly and enemy, WO Thompson and the division aviators all reported hundreds of civilian casualties resulting from indiscriminate troop firings; whereas LTC Barker and Capt. Medina reported a 128 VC body count and 20 civilians killed by artillery and gunships. This major dichotomy had to be sorted out by division headquarters.

When on 17 March MG Koster was informed of WO Thompson's observations he immediately ordered an investigation of the incident. The responsibility to investigate was given to Col. Henderson. Unbeknownst to Koster and Henderson, the two lower-level assault commanders, greatly concerned about the extent of civilian casualties, had initiated a cover-up whose purpose was to convince the two senior officers that the My Lai 4 assault had been a contested battle and 128 VC and 20 non-combatants had been killed. To their shame, the assault leaders boldly and repeatedly insisted verbally on those false facts and cleverly manipulated written reports to contain the same information. Unfortunately, Koster and Henderson believed the concocted story, which stated that 128 VC and 20 non-combatants were casualties. The cover-up was successful. The Americal Division Headquarters failed to determine the scope of the My Lai atrocities.

It appears that those most responsible for the Americal Division's failure to properly investigate and report the results of the My Lai assault were:

> LTC Barker (deceased) and Capt. Medina for their cover-up activities.
> Col. Henderson for negligently failing to properly investigate.
> BG Young and MG Koster for their "incredible mismanagement."

Medina and Henderson were court-martialed. However, the charges prepared against Medina failed to portray his actions with respect to the reporting and investigating of the My Lai affair. Medina, who along with Barker was primarily responsible for the My Lai cover-up, was charged for command actions taken on the ground during the assault and not for his cover-up activities. Henderson was charged for willfully failing to conduct a thorough investigation, that is, being complicit in the cover-up -- which he was not. Consequently both were found not guilty.

Young and Koster underwent Article 32 investigations which focused on their prior outstanding military service and not upon their gross mismanagement of the My Lai investigations and their charges were dismissed. LTG Peers was especially disturbed concerning the dismissal of charges against the senior officers and felt it was a travesty of justice.[1]

However, the Department of the Army on its review of the Peers Inquiry on 19 May 1971 determined that the Americal Division headquarters had mismanaged its efforts to report and investigate the My Lai 4 incident and the Secretary of the Army vacated Gen. Koster's rank of temporary major general, reducing him to his permanent rank of brigadier general and withdrew his Distinguished Service Medal. The Secretary of the Army also withdrew BG Young's Distinguished Service Medal and issued him a letter of censure.

This book has shown how the cover-up was orchestrated by LTC Barker, abetted by Capt. Medina and the troop's on the ground during the assault. When the cover-up within the division is understood for what it was -- those lower-level individuals involved in the assault attempting to mitigate knowledge of the slaughter -- then the Army's investigative conclusions can be considered reasonable. Koster and Henderson were not complicit in the cover-up but they had badly mismanaged the investigations of the varying field reports. When one considers the My Lai chain of command, all the officers, with the exception of LTC Barker who was killed in action, were either court-martialed or received punishment. The US Army acted responsibly by investigating the incident, publishing all the facts and attempting to punish those who it believed had committed criminal and military offenses.

Almost every aspect of the My Lai incident reflected poorly on the US Army: the killing of hundreds of Vietnamese non-combatants; the false reporting and deceit of Barker and Medina; the dysfunctional actions or lack of actions taken by the Americal Division staff; and the incompetence of the division's senior officers. However, the My Lai 4 travesty would have been much more damning if the Americal Division at every level had acted to suppress information of the atrocity as has erroneously been reported previously. This book has shown there was not a division-wide suppression of information.

EPILOGUE

Shortly after submitting the Report of Investigation, the investigating officer received a letter from Colonel Oran Henderson[101] stating he had received fair and impartial treatment and reaffirming his long held confidence and faith in the military judicial system. He went on to state:

> "General, this has been a most painful and depressing experience and I am eager not to dwell on it much longer, but regardless of your findings and recommendations which I am, of course not privy to at this time, I do want you to know that:
>
> I personally observed no atrocities.
>
> I had no knowledge, either directly or indirectly, of any cover-up or conspiracy.
>
> I never knowingly lied to the Peers Inquiry, Congressional Committee, CID, the 32 hearings of any other person in authority regarding this incident.
>
> I would under no circumstance perform any act of disloyalty to my Country, nor Army, nor my Soldiers.
>
> My single fault was a failure to ferret out the truth of what happened due probably to a lack of inquisitiveness.
>
> Providing the Army is willing, I plan very shortly to retire. I take this action reluctantly, however, with no sense of guilt or remorse, but rather with a feeling of full satisfaction in having served my Country to the best of my ability."

APPENDIX A

Phoenix, Arizona
March 29, 1969

Gentlemen:

It was late in April, 1968 that I first heard of "Pinkville" and what allegedly happened there. I received that first report with some skepticism, but in the following months I was to hear similar stories from such a wide variety of people that it became impossible for me to disbelieve that something rather dark and bloody did indeed occur sometime in March, 1968 in a village called "Pinkville" in the Republic of Viet Nam.

The circumstances that led to my having access to the reports I'm about to relate need explanation. I was inducted in March, 1967 into the U.S. Army. After receiving various training I was assigned to the 70th Infantry Detachment (LRP), 11th Light Infantry Brigade at Schofield Barracks, Hawaii, in early October, 1967. That unit, the 70th Infantry detachment (LRP), was disbanded a week before the 11th Brigade shipped out for Viet Nam on the 5th of December, 1967. All of the men from whom I later heard reports of the "Pinkville" incident were reassigned to Charlie Company, 1st Battalion, 20th Infantry, 11th Light Infantry Brigade. I was reassigned to the aviation section of Headquarters Headquarters Company 11th LIB. After we had been in Viet Nam for 3 to 4 months many of the men from the 70th Inf. Det. (LRP) began to transfer into the same unit, "E" Company, 51st Inf. (LRP).

In late April, 1968 I was awaiting orders for a transfer from HHC, 11th Brigade to Company "E", 51st Inf. (LRP), when I happened to run into Pfc Butch Gruver, whom I had known in Hawaii. Gruver told me he had been assigned to Charlie Company 1st of the 20th until April 1st when he transferred to the unit that I was headed for. During the course of our conversation he told me the first of many reports I was to hear of "Pinkville".

"Charlie" Company 1/20 had been assigned to Task Force Barker in late February, 1968 to help conduct "search and destroy" operations on the Batangan peninsula, Barker's area of operation. The task force was operating out of L.F. Dottie, located five or six miles north of Quang Ngai city on Vietnamese national highway 1. Gruver said that Charlie Company had sustained casualties; primarily from mines and booby traps, almost

153

every day from the first day they arrived on the peninsula. One village area was particularly troublesome and seemed to be infested with booby traps and enemy soldiers. It was located about six miles northeast of Quang Ngai city at approximate coordinates B.S. 728795. It was a notorious area and the men of Task Force Barker had a special name for it: they called it "Pinkville". One morning in the latter part of March, Task Force Barker moved out from its firebase headed for "Pinkville". Its mission: destroy the trouble spot and all of its inhabitants.

When "Butch" told me this I didn't quite believe that what he was telling me was true, but he assured me that it was and went on to describe what had happened. The other two companies that made up the task force cordoned off the village so that "Charlie" Company could move through to destroy the structures and kill the inhabitants. Any villagers who ran from Charlie Company were stopped by the encircling companies. I ask "Butch" several times if all the people were killed. He said that he thought they were, men, women and children. He recalled seeing small boy, about three or four years old, standing by the trail with a gunshot wound in one arm. The boy was clutching his wounded arm with his other hand, while blood trickled between his fingers. He was staring around himself in shock and disbelief at what he saw. "He just stood there with big eyes staring around like he didn't understand; he didn't believe what was happening. Then the captain's RTO (radio operator) put a burst of 16 (M-16 rifle) fire into him." It was so bad, Gruver said, that one of the men in his squad shot himself in the foot in order to be medevac-ed out of the area so that he would not have to participate in the slaughter. Although he had not seen it, Gruver had been told by people he considered trustworthy that one of the company's officers, 2nd Lieutenant Kally (this spelling may be incorrect) had rounded up several groups of villagers (each group consisting of a minimum of twenty persons of both sexes and all ages). According to the story, Kally then machine-gunned each group. Gruver estimated that the population of the village had been 300 to 400 people and that very few, if any, escaped.

After hearing this account I couldn't quite accept it. Somehow I just couldn't believe that not only had so many young American men participated in such an act of barbarism, but that their officers had ordered it. There were other men in the unit I was soon to be assigned to, "E" Company, 51st Infantry (LRP), who had been in Charlie Company at the time that Gruver alleged the incident at "Pinkville" had occurred. I became determined to ask them about "Pinkville" so that I might compare their accounts with Pfc Gruver's.

When I arrived at "Echo" Company, 51st Infantry (LRP) the first men I looked for were Pfc's Michael Terry and William Doherty. Both were veterans of "Charlie" Company, 1/20 and "Pinkville". Instead of contradicting "Butch" Gruver's story they corroborated it, adding some tasty tidbits of information of their own. Terry and Doherty had been in the same squad and their platoon was the third platoon of Charlie Company to pass through the village. Most of the people they came to were already dead. Those that weren't were sought out and shot. The platoon left nothing alive, neither livestock or people. Around noon the two soldiers' squad stopped to eat. "Billy and I started to get out our chow," Terry said, "But close to us was a bunch of Vietnamese in a heap, and some of them were moaning. Kally (2nd Lt. Kally) had been through before us and all of them had been shot, but many weren't dead. It was obvious that they weren't going to get any medical attention so Billy and I got up and went over to where they were. I guess we sort of finished them off." Terry went on to say that he and Doherty then returned to where their packs were and ate lunch. He estimated the size of the village to be 200 to 300 people. Doherty thought that the population of "Pinkville" had been 400 people.

If Terry, Doherty and Gruver could be believed, then not only had "Charlie" Company received orders to slaughter all the inhabitants of the village, but those orders had come from the commanding officer of Task Force Barker, or possibly even higher in the chain of command. Pfc Terry stated that when Captain Medina (Charlie Company's commanding officer Captain Ernest Medina) issued the order for the destruction of "Pinkville" he had been hesitant, as if it were something he didn't want to do but had to. Others I spoke to concurred with Terry on this.

It was June before I spoke to anyone who had something of significance to add to what I had already been told of the "Pinkville" incident. It was the end of June, 1968 when I ran into Sergeant Larry La Croix at the USO in Chu Lai. La Croix had been in 2nd Lt. Kally's platoon on the day Task Force Barker swept through "Pinkville". What he told me verified the stories of the others, but he also had something new to add. He had been a witness to Kally's gunning down of at least three separate groups of villagers. "It was terrible. They were slaughtering the villagers like so many sheep." Kally's men were dragging people out of bunkers and hooches and putting them together in a group. The people in the group were men, women and children of all ages. As soon as he felt that the group was big enough, Kally ordered an M-60 (machine-gun) set up and the people killed. La Croix said that he bore witness to this procedure at least three times. The three groups were of different sizes, one of about twenty people, one of about thirty people, and one of about forty people. When the first group was put together Kally ordered Pfc Torres to man the machine-gun and open fire on the villagers that had been grouped together. This Torres did, but before everyone in the group was down he ceased fire and refused to fire again. After ordering Torres to recommence firing several times, Lieutenant Kally took over the M-60 and finished shooting the remaining villagers in that first group himself. Sergeant La Croix told me that Kally didn't bother to order anyone to take the machine-gun when the other two groups of villagers were formed. He simply manned it himself and shot down all villagers in both groups.

This account of Sergeant La Croix's confirmed the rumors that Gruver, Terry and Doherty had previously told me about Lt. Kally. It also convinced me that there was a very substantial amount of truth to the stories that all of these men had told. If I needed more convincing, I was to receive it.

It was in the middle of November, 1968 just a few weeks before I was to return to the United States for separation from the army that I talked to Pfc Michael Bernhardt. Bernhardt had served his entire year in Viet Nam in "Charlie" Company 1/20 and he too was about to go home. "Bernie" substantiated the tales told by the other men I had talked to in vivid, bloody detail and added this. "Bernie" had absolutely refused to take part in the massacre of the villagers of "Pinkville" that morning and he thought that it was rather strange that the officers of the company had not made an issue of it. But that evening Medina (Captain Ernest Medina) came up to me ("Bernie") and told me not to do anything stupid like write my congressman" about what had happened that day. Bernhardt assured Captain Medina that he had no such thing in mind. He had nine months left in Viet Nam and felt that it was dangerous enough just fighting the acknowledged enemy.

Exactly what did, in fact, occur in the village of "Pinkville" in March, 1968 I do not know for certain, but I am convinced that it was something very black indeed. I remain irrevocably persuaded that if you and I do truly believe in the principles of justice and the equality of every man, however humble, before the law, that form the very backbone that this country is founded on, then we must press forward a widespread and public investigation of this matter with all our combined efforts. I think that it was Winston Churchill who once said "A country without a conscience is a country without a soul, and a country without a soul is a country that cannot survive." I feel that I must take some positive action on this matter. I hope that you will launch an investigation immediately and keep me informed of your progress. If you cannot, then I don't know what other course of action to take.

I have considered sending this to newspapers, magazines, and broadcasting companies, but I somehow feel that investigation and action by the Congress of the United States is the appropriate procedure, and as a conscientious citizen I have no desire to further besmirch the image of the American serviceman in the eyes of the world. I feel that this action, while probably it would promote attention, would not bring about the constructive actions that the direct actions of the Congress of the United States would.

Sincerely,

Ron Ridenhour

APPENDIX B
Abbreviations and Acronyms

NVA	North Vietnamese Army
GVN	Government of South Vietnam
RVNAF	Republic of Vietnam Armed Forces
ARVN	Army of South Vietnam
VC	Viet Cong
HES	Hamlet Evaluation System
MACV	Military Assistant Command of Vietnam
PF	Popular Forces
RF	Reginal Force
PSFD	People Self-Defense Force of South Vietnam
KIA	Killed in Action
AO	Area of Operation
LZ	Landing Zone
DZ	Drop Zone
CO	Commanding Officer
J-	Joint Level
G-	Division Level
S-	Battalion or Regiment Level
-2	Intelligence
-3	Operations
-4	Logistics
-5	Civil Affairs
Call Sign -6	Commander

BIBLIOGRAPHY

1.) LTG(Ret) W. R. Peers, The My Lai Inquiry, pages 207, 212, 225, 230; 1979, WW Norton, New York.

2.) Memorandum, Subject: Directive for Investigation, 26Nov1969, Sec. of the Army, Washington, D.C.

3.) Book, 10 U.S. Code Chapter 47, "United States Uniform Code of Military Justice", 2006, Washington, D.C.

4.) MG(Ret) I. A. Hunt Jr., The 9th Division in Vietnam, 2010, University Press of Kentucky, Lexington, KY

5.) BG(Ret) Tran Dinh Tho, Pacification, 1980, Indochina Memographs, US Army Center of Military History, Washington, D.C.

6.) Document, Hamlet Evaluation System, DAR R70-79, 1Sep1971, Hq MACV, Rep. of Vietnam

7.) Letter, Subject: Use of HES and TFES as Management Tools, 15May1968, Hq III MAF, Vietnam

8.) Directive Number 20-4, Subject: Inspections and Investigations, WAR CRIMES, 27Apr1967, MACV, Saigon, Vietnam

9.) Gen. Westmoreland, William C., Testimony before the Special Committee – Sony My, Committee on Armed Services, House of Representatives, Washington, D.C.

10.) BG Lipscomb, Andy, Testimony, Peers Inquiry, 23Jan1970, pages 5, 9, 10

11.) Col. Henderson, Oran K., Testimony, Peers Inquiry, 2Dec1969, page 30

12.) Fact Sheet, Subject: Company C, 1st Battalion, 20th Infantry, 12Jan1970, DA, OCSPER – CSD, Washington, D.C.

13.) LTC Beers, Edwin D., Testimony, Peers Inquiry, 11Dec1970, page 563

14.) Small, John H., Sworn Statement, 14Dec1969, Renton, Washington

15.) J-2, Joint General Staff, Republic of Vietnam Armed Forces, "Communists Assessment of the RVNAF", Saigon, 1973

16.) SFC Stephens, Clinton D., Testimony, Henderson Article 32, 28Aug1970, page 121

17.) Col. Henderson, Oran K., Testimony, Henderson Article 32, 16Dec1970, pages 647-648, 664-682, 679, 695-714, 763-806, 844-845, 876, 901-907, 984

18.) Capt. Vasquez, Dennis R., Testimony, Henderson Article 32, 25Sep1970, pages 287-290

19.) Capt. Kotouc, Eugene M., Testimony, Henderson Article 32, 25Sep1970, page 278

20.) Creswell, Carl Edward, Sworn Statement, 11Dec1969, Emporia, KS

21.) SEC Cowan, Isaiah, Testimony, Peers Inquiry, 18Dec1969, page 10

22.) Pvt. Kinch, Thomas, Testimony, Henderson Article 32, 28Aug1970, pages 131-133

23.) Capt. Medina, Ernest L., Testimony, Peers Inquiry, 4Dec1969, pages 7-8, 15-27, 35-44, 61-66

24.) Flynn, James H., Testimony, Peers Inquiry, 6Mar1970, pages 2, 16-18

25.) SSG Bacon, L.G., Testimony, Peers Inquiry, 16Dec1969

26.) Sgt. Hutson, Max D., Testimony, Peers Inquiry, 28Oct1969

27.) Specialist Carter, Herbert L., Testimony, Peers Inquiry, 2Jan1970, pages 26, 48

28.) Sgt. Bernhardt, Michael A., Testimony, Peers Inquiry, 29Dec1969, page 24

29.) Specialist Widmer, Cedrick J., Testimony, Peers Inquiry, 29Dec1969, page 24

30.) SP5 Flores, Abel, Testimony, Peers Inquiry, 3Feb1970, pages 30, 31

31.) Cpl. Kern, William H., Testimony, Peers Inquiry, 31Jan1970, page 20

32.) SP4 Sledge, Charles, Testimony, Peers inquiry, 8Jan1970, page 37

33.) Pfc. Bunning, Dennis M., Testimony, Peers Inquiry, 16Jan1970, page 52

34.) Pfc. Moss, Tommy, Testimony, Peers Inquiry, 5Jan1970, page 29

35.) Pfc. Pendleton, Richard W., Testimony, Peers Inquiry, 23Jan1970, pages 27, 28

36.) Conti, Dennis I., Testimony, Peers Inquiry, 2Jan1970, pages 28-44

37.) Article, "The Massacre at My Lai", Life Magazine, Vol. 67, No. 23, December 5, 1969

38.) Hersh, Seymour M., Article, "A Report of the Massacre and its Aftermath, My Lai 4", Harper's Magazine, May 1970, NY, NY

39.) 1stSGT Buchanon, Jay A., Testimony, Henderson Article 32, 24Sep1970, page 270

40.) Sgt. Fagan, Martin E., Testimony, Henderson Article 32, 11Sep1970, pages 226-227

41.) Moody, John W., Testimony, Henderson Article 32, 4Dec1970, pages 548-553

42.) Haeberle, Ronald L., Testimony, Henderson Article 32, 10Oct1970, pages 294-304

43.) LTC Luper, Robert V., Testimony, Henderson Article 32, 10Dec1969, pages 139-149

44.) LTC Luper, Robert V., Testimony, Peers inquiry, 3Sep1970, pages 4, 8, 9, 36, 94, 100

45.) Capt. Gamble, Steven J., Testimony, Peers Inquiry, 1970, pages 3-5, 11-18, 31

46.) Alaux Jr., Roger L., Testimony, Peers Inquiry, 6Jan1970, pages 14-19, 86-101

47.) McCrary, Lanny J., Testimony, Peers Inquiry, pages 2-29, 46-60

48.) Doersam, Russell E., Testimony, Peers Inquiry, 24Jan1970, pages 9-17, 32-45

49.) 1stLt. Thompson, Hugh C., Testimony, Henderson Article 32, 27Aug1970, pages 107-114, 117-130

50.) Maj. Watke, Frederick W., Testimony, Peers Inquiry, 8,11Dec1969, pages 8-17

51.) WO Culverhouse, Jerry R., Testimony, Henderson Article 32, 21Aug1970 and 24Sep1970, pages 63-70, 267-269

52.) WO Mansell, Charles H., Testimony, Peers Inquiry, 24Dec1969

53.) Col. Henderson, Oran K., Testimony, Peers Inquiry, 2Dec1969, page 35, 12Dec1969, page 161, 19Dec1969, page 253-254, 13Feb1970, 16Feb1970, 17Feb1970

54.) Maj. McKnight, Robert W., Testimony, Peers Inquiry, 3Dec1969, pages 9-13, 41, 50

55.) LTC MacLachlan, William I., Testimony, Henderson Article 32, 3Dec1970, pages 527-532

56.) Adcock, Michael C., Testimony, Peers Inquiry, 5Nov1970

57.) Capt. Cooney, James T., Testimony, Henderson Article 32, 4Dec1970, pages 537-544

58.) Capt. Lewellen, Charles R., Testimony, Henderson Article 32, 11Sep1970, pages 232-234

59.) Sgt. Watson, William E., Testimony, Henderson Article 32, 10Sep1970, 208-210

60.) Capt. Moe, Thelmer A., Testimony, Henderson Article 32, 4Sep1970, pages 181-184

61.) Kubert, Lawrence J., Testimony, Henderson Article 32, 6Oct1970, page 308

62.) Roberts, Randell, Testimony, Peers Inquiry, 17Jan1970

63.) CSM Kirkpatric, Roy D., Testimony, Henderson Article 32, 4Sep1970, page 166

64.) CSM Rogers, James D., Testimony, Henderson Article 32, 4Sep1970, page 155

65.) LTC Holladay, John L., Testimony, Henderson Article 32, 27Aug1970, pages 95-101

66.) BG Young, George H., Testimony, Henderson Article 32, 20Aug1970, pages 4-6

67.) LTC(Chaplain) Lewis, Francis R., Testimony, Henderson Article 32, 10Sep1970, pages 187-191

68.) MG Koster, Samuel W., Testimony, Koster Article 32, 22Sep1970, pages 1-158

69.) Report, LTC Frank A. Barker Jr., Subject: Combat Action Report (RCS AVDF-GC1), 28Mar1968, Hq TFB, Americal Division, Vietnam

70.) Roberts, Jay Alfred, Sworn Statement, 12Sep1969, Washington, D.C.

71.) Cadreman Phong Duc, Letter, Subject: Republic of Vietnam Letter Report, 18Mar1968, CSG, Vietnam

72.) 1st Lt. Tran Ngoc Tan, Letter, Subject: Confirmation of Allied Troops Shooting at the Residents of Tuo Cung Hamlet, Coordinates BS721795, 28Mar1968, Son Tinh District, Quang Ngai Province, Vietnam

73.) 1ˢᵗLt. Tran Ngoc Tan, Letter, Subject: Allied Operation at Son My Assembled and Killed Civilians, 11Apr1968, Son Tinh District, Quang Ngai Province, Vietnam

74.) Capt. Angel M. Rodriquez, Statement, reference letter from Son Tinh District Chief to the Quang Ngai Province Chief, Subject: Allied Forces Gathered People of Son My Village for Killing, dated 11Apr1968, District Advisor Son Tinh District, Quang Ngai Province, Vietnam

75.) Rodriquez, Angel M., Testimony, Peers Inquiry, 6Sep1970, pages 10-12, 52, 129

76.) Hill, John W., Sworn Statement, 14Oct1970, Denver, CO

77.) VC Propaganda Message, Subject: Concerning the Crimes Committed by US Imperialists and Their lackeys who Killed More than 500 Civilians of Tinh Khe(V), Son Tinh(B), 28Mar1968, National Liberation Front of Quang Ngai Province, Vietnam

78.) Letter, Subject: Safeguarding of All Non-combatants, 24Mar1968, Hq. Americal Division, Vietnam

79.) Col. Parsons, Nels A., Testimony, Henderson Article 32, 21Aug1970

80.) Col. Trexler, Tommy P., Testimony, Henderson Article 32, 3Sep1970, pages 150-154

81.) Col. Balmer, Jesmond D., Testimony, Henderson Article 32, 26Aug1970, pages 86-93

82.) Anistranski, Charles, Testimony, Peers Inquiry, 12Jan1970, pages 3-30

83.) Capt. Keshel, Donald J., Testimony, Henderson Article 32, 3Dec1970, pages 524-525

84.) Col. Jones, John T., Testimony, Peers Inquiry, 19Dec1969, pages 5, 6

85.) Maj. Comeau, Robert F., Testimony, Henderson Article 32, 11Dec1970, pages 571-575

86.) Col. Hetherly, James, Testimony, Peers Inquiry, 20Jan1970

87.) LTC Lucas, Warren J., Testimony, Henderson Article 32, 26Aug1970, pages 79-81

88.) Blackledge, Richard K., Testimony, Henderson Article 32, 3Dec1970, pages 500-516

89.) 1ˢᵗLt. Thompson, Hugh C., Testimony, Peers Inquiry, 3Dec1969, pages 16-20, 91-93

90.) Maj. Calhoun, Charles G., Sworn Statement, 15Jan1970, Fort Monroe, VA

91.) Maj. Gibson, Glenn D., Testimony, Henderson Article 32, 24Aug1970, pages 74-76

92.) Riggs, William C., Sworn Statement, 14Jan1970, Midland, TX

93.) Pittman, John L., Sworn Statement, 5Dec1969, Fort Gordon, GA

94.) CSM Walsh, Joseph W., Testimony, Henderson Article 32, 3Dec1970, page 536

95.) MSG Gross, Russell V., Sworn Statement, 20Aug1970, Fort Knox, KY

96.) Colburn, Lawrence M., Deposition, 27Oct1970, Algona, WA

97.) DiFilippo Jr., Michael, Testimony, Henderson Article 32, 24Sep1970, page 263

98.) LTC Brannen Jr., Barney L., Testimony, Henderson Article 32, 10Sep1970

99.) Letter, Col. Oran K. Henderson to Gen. Westmoreland, dated 10Dec1969, Norfolk, VA

100.) Letter, Subj: "Advice on Disposition of Court Martial Charges", 20Feb1971, HQ, 1st US Army, Fort Meade, MD

101.) Letter, Colonel Oran K. Henderson to BG Ira A. Hunt, 18Feb1971, Norfolk, VA

102.) Holbrook, Richard J., Sworn Statement 10Sep1970, Orlando, FL

103.) Wilson, Clyde P., Sworn Statement 21Jan1970, Alamorgordo, NM

104.) 1SGT Saimons, Mich E., Testimony, Henderson Article 32, 26Aug1970, page 52

105.) Report, Review of the Preliminary Investigations into the My Lai Incident, Vol. 1, 14Mar1970, Dept. of the Army, Washington, D.C.

106.) Book, Wright, James, "Enduring Vietnam: An American Generation and Its War", St. Martin's Press, New York, 2017, page 301

107.) Book, Bilton, Michael and Sim, Kevin, Four Hours in My Lai, 1992, Penguin Group, NY, NY

108.) TV, PBS.org/WGBH/American Experience, My Lai Massacre

109.) Stanley, Harry Sworn Statement 14Oct1969, Long Beach, CA

111.) Sgt. Olsen, Gregory Thomas, Sworn Statement, 30Aug1969, Fort Lewis, WA

112.) Capt. Medina, Ernest L., Discussions at the Henderson Article 32, 15Oct1970, Fort Meade, MD

113.) Book, Ricks, Thomas E., <u>The Generals</u>, 2012, Penguin Books, New York, NY

114.) Congressman Stratton, Samuel S., Documented Speech, House of Representatives, 4 Feb 1971, Washington, D.C.

www.ingramcontent.com/pod-product-compliance
Lightning Source LLC
Chambersburg PA
CBHW051426090426
42737CB00014B/2846